DEMONS

OF

POVERTY

DEMONS OF POVERTY

one entrepreneur's experience with addressing poverty in Haiti

TED BOERS and TIM STONER

with contributions from

JAN BOERS

ISBN 978-1-942503-57-6

ACTON INSTITUTE

98 E. Fulton
Grand Rapids, Michigan 49503
616.454.3080
www.acton.org

Interior design: Beth Shagene
Cover design: Peter Ho

Printed in the United States of America

*It has been said that as many as twenty percent
of Haitians have left Haiti in the last forty years
to seek a better life in the United States,
France, Canada and other countries.*

*This book is dedicated to the Haitians
I have met who have the option to leave
but made the decision to stay
so that they could make a difference.
You know who you are.*

Contents

SPIRITUAL REFLECTIONS

PRACTICAL REFLECTIONS

APPENDICES

Acknowledgments

MY WRITING STYLE IS TO MAKE NOTES ABOUT WHAT I AM learning on this journey we call life. Sometimes those notes end up in my journal, sometimes they end up in a topical index and sometimes they end up in the wastepaper basket. My ten-year Haitian journey resulted in a lot of notes.

I would like to thank my wife Jan for encouraging me to share my Haiti notes so that others can hopefully learn from them. I would also like to thank her for encouraging me along the way and for making her own unique contribution to this book.

I would like to thank Tim Stoner for helping me to take hundreds of pages of these notes and turning them into a story.

I would also like to thank friends of mine who walked parts of this story with me and who were then kind enough to read the manuscript and offer their thoughts and suggestions. For this I am indebted to Marc Andreas, Dave Arnold, Tim Berends, Trish Borgdorff, Mike Buwalda, Tim Cole, Henry Doorn, Dave Genzink, Jon Genzink, Chris Jensen, Lesly Jules, Jonathan Loux, Rob Petroelje, Doug Seebeck, David Tigchelaar and Robert Ulysse.

Foreword

FOR AS LONG AS I CAN REMEMBER HAITI HAS BEEN REFERRED to as the poorest country in the Western Hemisphere. Thousands of international NGOs (Non-Government Organizations) and tens of thousands of people have been at work for decades trying to improve the quality of life for the Haitian people. During this time billions of dollars of international aid was invested in this country. And yet, even before the 2010 earthquake, Haiti was still considered to be the poorest country in the Western Hemisphere.

For ten years (2002 – 2011) I was one of those people trying to make a difference in Haiti. This book is about my experiences. From these experiences I draw some conclusions and some lessons. My hope is that they will be helpful to the thousands who are devoting themselves to improving the quality of life for the people of Haiti and the millions of others in similar impoverished areas of the world. You may not agree with all of my conclusions. That is okay. However, it is my hope that this book will stimulate a fair and respectful conversation, one from which we will all be able to learn.

Ten years ago I had the boldness and the audacity to tell Haitian people what they should do to improve their lot in life and to tell Americans what they should do to help the Haitian people.

I don't anymore.
I have learned some of what I did not know.
That is what this book is about.

TED BOERS
2012

About the Author

TED BOERS WAS BORN IN THE NETHERLANDS IN 1946. HIS PARents immigrated to Canada in 1952. As was the case with most immigrant families, Ted's family experienced relative poverty for many years. However, since most of his peers were in a similar situation, the experience of poverty was not particularly traumatic. Ted came to the United States in 1964 to attend Calvin College in Grand Rapids Michigan. One semester was prepaid as a result of a summer job and a small scholarship and he had $20 in his pocket that his mother had given him.

Ted started his business career while still in college, selling everything from strawberries to encyclopedias and a legal pepper spray that could be used for self-defense. During his college years he also worked for the Fatman International Private Detective Agency putting a healthy fear into straying husbands.

It was at Calvin College that Ted met Jan who was from Highland, Indiana. They married in 1968. During the next eight years three children were born who in turn have added eight delightful grandchildren to the family.

Upon graduating from Calvin College, Ted went to work for a large Insurance Company. The corporate world felt constraining so he left after five years. This turned out to be a false start into his own entrepreneurial career so he returned to the same insurance company for five more years. This time he left for good, starting seven different businesses over a period of twenty-five years. Today he continues to be the majority owner of two of these businesses.

Ted learned that starting businesses was difficult and time consuming but he also learned that once the business was on its' feet it could be very rewarding and liberating. That is what he wanted; time to do what he wanted to do. As he evaluated his options, it became clear that what he really wanted to do was to help other people who had not been as fortunate as he had been.

By 1993 Ted had accomplished his goal of freedom of time. He bought his first sailboat, which he and Jan enjoy sailing on Lake Michigan and he started a financial counseling ministry at his local church. This ministry gave Ted the opportunity to council many couples who were struggling with their finances and it led to various opportunities for public speaking in local churches as well as churches throughout the United States and Canada. After ten years of focus on stewardship and financial counseling, Ted wrote a book in an attempt to share what he had learned about stewardship and finance. The book is called *Three Simple Rules ... Guaranteed to Improve Your Financial Situation.*

By the year 2000, Ted's journey had evolved from helping local people with their finances to wondering about poverty issues on an international scale. That raised the question of who are the poor of the 21st century? It was that question that started the journey described in this book.

The Vision

As I walked along the beach I had a vision.
And in this vision I saw the Spirit of God
hovering over the country of Haiti.
The Spirit saw the squalor, the anguish
and the poverty of the Haitian people.
The Spirit saw the sick old man who had no medicine,
the poverty-stricken parents who had no job
and the hungry little girl who had no food.
And the Spirit of God was grieved and the Spirit's heart was broken.
As the Spirit of God shifted focus slightly to the west,
Miami came into view and then the entire state of Florida,
followed by Atlanta, Chicago and then
Grand Rapids, my hometown.
The Spirit of God saw the wealth, the affluence and the abundance
of the people in Miami, Atlanta, Chicago and Grand Rapids.
The Spirit saw the retired old man driving to the golf course
in his BMW, parents showering guilt presents on their children,
and the little girl competing in a beauty contest.
And again the Spirit of God was grieved
and again the Spirit's heart was broken.
This is not the way it is supposed to be.
Aren't there over 2000 verses in my Holy Book
that tell those who have,
to share with those who have not?
Don't they know?
Don't they care?

TED BOERS
March 2008

Prologue

THAT FRIGID MORNING IN 2008, I ARRIVED IN MY OFFICE IN Grand Rapids, Michigan unaware that I was about to receive a telephone call that would undermine everything I believed about God, and much of what I believed about myself. It would precipitate a crisis of faith that would last for almost three years; one that would challenge some of my core assumptions and bring hidden weaknesses into the light. And it would mark me indelibly. It was January 30, 2008.

For almost three years I had invested in and led the Nouveau Kiskeya (New Haiti) Development Project in Northwest Haiti. We were a group of American investors committed to developing fifteen miles of pristine ocean-front property about 100 miles north of Port-au-Prince. Our primary objective was to start a tax-free trade zone that would create thousands of jobs and help transform the neediest area of the poorest country in the Western Hemisphere. Our model would be the one that had put the Bahamas on the map 50 years earlier.

It was an ambitious project with a primarily philanthropic motive. As Christian business people whom God had prospered, we were all in agreement that a profitable return on investment was secondary to the goals of providing jobs for thousands and introducing them to the God of the Bible. The Nouveau Kiskeya Project was driven by a vision I was convinced God had prompted and repeatedly affirmed. I kept track of the miraculous interventions that supported the conclusion that this was a "God-project" which He had stamped with His seal of approval.

My involvement in Haiti had begun almost seven years earlier. It had not been easy. I, as well as others, had invested a significant amount of money and enormous amounts of time in business and political strategies that had not achieved the results we had anticipated. But the Nouveau Kiskeya project was different. As I walked into my office on that snowy morning, the "Miracle List," what I took to be miraculous affirmations of our development project, numbered sixteen. They reinforced my belief that, unlike those earlier attempts, this one could not fail.

I was about to begin a journey that almost cost me my faith. It would take several more years of my life, but painfully and ever-so-slowly, I was able to distill a handful of lessons I wish I had known at the beginning.

CHAPTER 1

Wanting to Make a Difference

I SUPPOSE I COULD BLAME IT ALL ON A BOOK I READ EARLY in 1998, *Half Time*, authored by Bob Buford. I was in my early 50's. I was CEO of Datacomp, a company I started in 1987 specializing in manufactured home appraisals. At the time we had 80 employees and about 3,000 independent-contractors all across the country. It was obvious that God had significantly blessed our business. Buford's book brought me up short and caused me to take appraisal of my own life. It prompted me to ask an important question, "God, what is it that you want me to do with the second half of my life?"

I had time and some money that could be used to make a difference somewhere. The "somewhere" that I believe God impressed on me was the island-nation of Haiti. I had never been there and didn't know much about it other than that it was extremely poor. I did remember seeing a picture of the Haitian President, Baby Doc Duvalier, I think it was on the cover of Time Magazine. I recalled news reports that had characterized Papa Doc and his son Baby Doc as ruthless dictators who had stolen millions from the national treasury. That was the extent of my knowledge about Haiti.

I knew I wanted to invest my energies and resources in a country I could get my head around. Since Haiti is the poorest nation in the Western hemisphere, but no bigger than Vermont, it seemed to fit the bill. It wasn't long after this that Kristin, our 22-year-old daughter, announced that she would be taking her Calvin College Interim course overseas. Coincidentally, the country she had chosen was Haiti. This was intriguing since, up until that moment, I had not mentioned my interest to anyone except my wife, Jan. My parting words to Kristin were: "Why don't you look around to see what a business guy like me might be able to do to help the people of Haiti."

When Kristin returned three weeks later, she told me that while in country she had heard of an organization committed to mobilizing Christian businesspeople called Partners for Christian Development (now Partners Worldwide). She suggested that I call them since she had been told that they were committed to starting businesses in Haiti.

I called Partners and learned that their mission coincided surprisingly with what I hoped to accomplish. A few days later Mike Buwalda, their development director, came to my office. He explained that the role of the organization was to introduce American businesspeople to struggling entrepreneurs in underdeveloped countries. The objective was to link the American businesspeople with these entrepreneurs to help them start or expand their business. Business growth would create jobs and allow the currently unemployed to become self-supporting. I was intrigued since that seemed like a great way for a businessperson like me to help the poor.

The problem was that Haiti was in a period of political instability and travel there was considered unadvisable. I waited for conditions to improve and a few years later, in 2002, I received the call from Partners asking if I was still interested in going to Haiti. I was. I made the arrangements and flew to Port-au-Prince, Haiti in February 2003. Despite the dirt, the crowds and the overwhelming poverty I felt an odd sense of excitement. I took it as an affirmation that I was exactly where I was supposed to be.

I was introduced to a number of Haitians who were leading the Partners' initiatives in Haiti and we quickly became friends. This was the opposite of what I had felt on a trip to Ecuador, several years earlier, in which I felt like an observer the entire time. In Haiti there was an almost instantaneous bond. This surprised me, for despite some discomfort resulting from the stark differences between the Haitian culture and my own, I was completely at home.

After meeting these key Haitian leaders, seeing their commitment and energy as well as the immense opportunities for business, I bought into the Partners Worldwide vision. I fully embraced their strategy of helping small business owners in Haiti succeed. When I returned home, Jan and I agreed immediately to support the start of their business incubator to help promote small business growth in Port-au-Prince.

During the next 18 months I would travel to Haiti three times. Early on we also decided to provide loans to a modest building-supply storeowner and to a lady selling handmade organic soaps at the airport. I mentored and encouraged these entrepreneurs, hoping to help them expand their business using the principles that had helped me. Slowly these experiences taught me my first crucial cross-cultural lesson. I did not know it at the time, but it is the one that laid the foundation for every lesson that would follow: doing business in an underdeveloped country is extraordinarily difficult.

Entrepreneurs face challenges everywhere but the difficulty factor increases exponentially in a country such as Haiti. Doing business there is not at all like doing business in the United States. My unexamined assumption before I ever touched the tarmac of the Port-au-Prince airport was that the principles that helped me succeed in Michigan would do the same for any Haitian who was willing to listen and work hard to implement them. After several trips I came to the realization that I had been wrong. Just because something works in the United States does not mean it will necessary work in an under-developed-world context.

I discovered that what makes it so incredibly difficult to succeed is the almost complete lack of infrastructure that we take for granted in the developed world. The roads are a disaster, water and electricity are erratic, and the justice system is frequently non-existent or corrupt. Nelson, one of the entrepreneurs Partners was helping, had to get up in the middle of the night to take advantage of a periodic two-hour electricity-window to power his tools in his small woodworking shop. In addition, assuming you were one of the few lucky ones who qualified for a loan, interest rates were averaging an exorbitant 35%.

By the end of 2004, after several years of effort and thousands of dollars in loans, I was ready to give up. I had tried all the conventional methods for business growth without seeing any results. There had been no appreciable increase in sales much less creation of new jobs, and as a result the loans were not being repaid. Worse, there was no evidence that either those who had received these funds or their employees were any better off.

Like a persistent mosquito, a question began pestering me: "Why doesn't anything seem to work in this country?" I had begun with such high hopes and had responded to what I believed was a call from God. Yet I was being forced to the disheartening conclusion that what we were doing was not working. While I was not prepared to give up on "my call" to the country, I was ready to quit trying to create jobs there.

Earlier that year God had given Jan and me an opportunity to start a children's ministry in Haiti. The seed of that ministry was actually planted during my first trip in 2003. The first Haitian I had met after arriving in the capital was Lesly Jules, Haitian Partnership Manager for Partners Worldwide. Lesly introduced me to his fiancée, Kerline Toussaint; a beautiful but very shy, young Haitian woman. Shortly thereafter Lesly and Kerline were married.

As Jan and I got to know this dedicated young couple, we learned that Kerline was on a mission to improve her English. To help her, we invited her to live in our home in West

Michigan for three months in early 2004. Every evening over dinner, we found ourselves talking about her homeland. During one of these conversations Jan and I shared that we had been thinking about helping Haitian orphans. Kerline looked at us in shock. She told us that she actually had plans in her briefcase for starting an orphanage. She had been working on them for about two years while employed by a Baptist mission organization.

As we discussed the details, Kerline began to explain that many orphans in Haiti are not really orphans, since many of them have one or two living parents. She also introduced us to a culturally ingrained system we had never heard of. "There is something we call *restavec*," she said. It is a term that comes from a delightfully innocent French phrase, *reste avec*, "one who stays with" and conveys the imagery of someone enjoying a friend's warm hospitality.

However, the reality is much different. It is actually a cruel system that is so old and so woven into the culture it is almost invisible. As Kerline spoke, it became clear that *restavec* is a perverse euphemism for a system masquerading as hospitality but which frequently is actually nothing less than child abuse and child slavery.

Parents unable to care for their children leave them in the hands of families who are slightly higher on the economic ladder. These families promise to provide food, lodging and education in exchange for "light housework." In reality it is rarely that simple. Many of these children, as young as three or four years old, find themselves living in hovels in the back yard, and earn their keep by exhausting labor. Abuse is common. Education is frequently an ephemeral dream.

Oddly, what most struck Jan and I was Kerline's demeanor as she spoke. It was as if she were discussing Haitian weather patterns. Though a committed, college-educated Christian, she gave no indication that she recognized the depth of this systemically evil system.

When you grow up with a pervasive wickedness, education and Christianity are frequently not enough to give a clear perspective. Take slavery in our own country. How many "God-fearing" Christians recognized the horror and degradation they had grown comfortable with in their own towns, schools, and places of business? Separate drinking fountains and forbidden counters, along with designated bus seats were tolerated and supported by Christians in the United States for decades. Cultural paradigms are very dangerous things.

In June of 2004, we decided to respond by launching an organization called Rescue One. Kerline would be in charge. Her primary role was to encourage Haitian pastors to preach against this abusive system and take action against it. Rescue One Haiti would then be tasked with forming church partnerships that would reach out to the poorest of the poor children in their neighborhoods. The Haitian church partners would look for the most vulnerable, and the most desperate children. The Haitian church would make arrangements to provide Christian education, food, clothes, healthcare and summer spiritual retreats for the children. They would also be responsible for covering 10% of the cost, with the understanding that their percentage would increase a little bit every year. Rescue One USA would cover the remainder, which amounted to about $1000 per child per year.

That first year Rescue One, with the help of one local church, rescued 15 children. Today there are five churches that have joined hands to help 75 beautiful children. Local Haitian churches are finding strength and courage they did not know they had. And they are now paying an average of 30% of the program costs. One of the Haitian pastors expressed his gratitude that Rescue One had not followed the standard NGO model. "You have empowered us," he said. "You have allowed us to make the rules, you've let us lead and decide how the ministry should be run."

Some of the Haitian Church committee members made this remarkable admission: "we never understood that there were others we had a responsibility to serve. We were used to thinking of ourselves as recipients of charity. It did not occur to us that there were others who were needier than ourselves." (For more information about Rescue One check out the website at www.rescue-one.org.)

Although I was pleased with the success of the Rescue One effort I was still wrestling with unanswerable questions. After all, I was a businessman, my vocation was business, and my experience was in business. I knew the power for good that business and job opportunities could exert on people and communities, and how it could elevate the poor from despair to hope. I could not make sense of my inability to promote business growth and job-creation among people who were so crushed by poverty and had such a strong desire to break free from it.

In late 2004, as I was reevaluating our job creation efforts in Haiti, Partners Worldwide asked me to join them on a trip to help review the progress of the business incubator which had been started two years earlier. I didn't really want to go. My experiences had convinced me that it would be unproductive.

Several days later, as I was struggling to make up my mind, I came across a one-page article written by a researcher at the UN. It was about the UN's prognosis for Haiti for the next ten years. One sentence in particular blew me away: "Haiti appears to be headed toward another decade of decline, with health, education and social services suffering amid continuing conflict and environmental disaster."

How could this be? I wondered. How could life possibly get worse in what was already the poorest country in the Western Hemisphere? And why weren't the billions in aid and finances, provided by the international community, reversing this trend?

I thought about that for several days. I could not get those questions out of my mind. Then I began to write. I believed then and I believe now that God prompted what I wrote. A new strategy began to take shape. In hindsight, I recognize that it was a macro-approach to poverty-alleviation rather than the micro-approach on which I had been focused. Its central thrust was that American Christians had an opportunity and a responsibility to help their Haitian brothers and sisters make systemic changes in their country.

These thoughts turned into a three-page letter to Doug Seebeck, the Executive Director of Partners Worldwide. In it I stated my conviction that "this continuing deteriorating Haitian situation demands a Christian response" and asked him if he would be willing to join me on a "preposterous journey."

I went on to say that "I believe it's time for the Christian community to step to the plate. Our choice is simple: we can continue to dabble in Haiti and allow millions of people, right in the backyard of the largest and richest Christian country in the world, to live and die in abject poverty; or we can rise to the occasion and begin to act as if the lives of our Haitian brothers and sisters depended on it — because it does!"

The strategy was simple: the North American Christian community would do everything it could to help Haitians establish a Christian government and provide assistance to stabilize its economy. This is where the plan became audacious. Economic stability would be accomplished by creating a Free Trade Zone that would offer employment to at least 100,000 Haitians by the end of 2007, and a million jobs by the end of the decade.

Doug's response was not only positive but enthusiastic. In addition, our friends in Haiti without hesitation and with great excitement affirmed this idea. Two weeks later I was invited to speak at a rally of Haitian Christians inside the National Palace in Port-au-Prince. It appeared that God was opening doors. We were on a roll.

If a man shuts his ears to the cry of the poor,
he too will cry out and not be answered.

PROVERBS 21:13   *Amen !*

CHAPTER 2

God Opens Doors

WHAT WE DID NOT KNOW UNTIL WE ARRIVED IN PORT-AU-Prince was that our trip happened to coincide with a major conference taking place in the capital sponsored by Promise Keepers and several other national Christian organizations. The gathering was called Haiti at the Cross.

The preparation for this conference had begun long before I had written the letter to Doug Seebeck. When we found out what was converging in the capital we concluded that God had been at work preparing the way ahead of us.

At the rally in the National Palace on Thursday, December 9, 2004, approximately 500 of the most influential Christians in Haiti were in attendance. I was introduced to many Christian political leaders, including Chavannes Jeune, a Baptist pastor, who was running for President. We were told that a grass-roots Christian constituency that consisted of 40% of the Haitian population was supporting Mr. Jeune. Confident that God had been orchestrating affairs long before we showed up, we agreed to do everything we could to help elect Christians to national political office, including the Presidency. The elections were scheduled for November 13, 2005; one year away. I was encouraged.

However, we soon learned that Haitian Christians were not as excited about political solutions to their country's problems as we Americans were. To our surprise, many were not even registered to vote. The entrenched mentality among Haitian Christians, encouraged by several generations of missionaries, was that "earth is not my home, I'm a citizen of heaven." Politics was viewed as dirty and evil and the role of the Christian was to avoid its pollution and prepare for heaven. It would take several years before I recognized this to be an evangelical twist on a pervasive culture of passivity that dominates the nation of Haiti. It would take even longer before I began to understand the profoundly spiritual roots of this disabling mindset. Back then I did not give it a thought, speeding by these yellow lights, brimming with confidence that we had put together a feasible plan that could disprove the UN's pessimistic forecast.

Although the strong support from our Haitian friends seemed to indicate that we were moving in the right direction, I wanted to make certain that it was God who was behind these events. I told Doug Seebeck that before I agreed to forge ahead, I needed one final indicator. This last confirmation would be a face-to-face meeting between Mr.

Chavannes Jeune, the Haitian candidate for President, and Mr. Rich DeVos, billionaire co-founder of AMWAY Global, a Partners board member and Doug Seebeck's mentor.

Two months later, on January 26, 2005, the introductions took place at the Ritz Carlton Hotel in Palm Beach, Florida. God had answered our prayers. One of the invitees was Robert Ulysse, a Haitian specializing in international relations. He was a friend and confidant of Mr. Jeune. He had served in the Cabinet of the Haitian interim Prime Minister Gerard Latortue in 2004 after the ouster of President Jean-Bertrand Aristide. Neither one of us was aware that the most significant event that day was our meeting, an item that did not show up on the agenda.

Seventy-eight-year-old Rich DeVos walked into the room tanned and in good shape. He did not betray any weakness from his heart-transplant eight years earlier. After some preliminary remarks, he looked directly at me and asked: "How can I help you?" Our conversation lasted 2½ hours and when it was over we left with his agreement to support Haiti for Christ, the name we had selected for the grand design to help Haitians rebuild Haiti from the top down. Having received the confirmation I was looking for I concluded that God was behind our plans for a re-structured and prosperous Haiti. As a result, I fully committed and 2005 turned into my political year.

In order to mobilize the evangelical voting block, our first priority was to provide materials that would explain the biblical basis for engagement in the political process. These materials would be distributed through all the Protestant churches. The goal was to break down their historic repugnance for what they considered to be the corrupt business of politics.

Robert Ulysse, who I had met for the first time in our meeting with Mr. DeVos, was to be our civic education consultant and was tasked to translate the instructional manual into French and Creole. Only later did I learn that it was due to his long friendship with Mr. Jeune that he had set aside his strong reservations about the viability of a united evangelical electorate and agreed to join the team. Soon he had helped distribute thousands of copies of the civics manual written for us by former missionary Dirk Oostendorp. It was entitled Espoir pour Haiti (Hope for Haiti).

My optimism was fueled by the support of Christians in the U.S., and by the encouragement of Haitian leaders, both in-country and in the Diaspora. This lasted for five months. In July of 2005 this optimism came to an abrupt end and my excitement turned to dismay.

The race for president included a diverse field of 35 candidates. While this sounds like a confusing mob by North American standards, I had been assured that this was about average in Haitian politics so the numbers did not concern me. However, in the middle of the summer I made a distressing discovery: Mr. Jeune was not the only Christian in the race. He was actually one of three, all competing for the same office.

Due to the large number of candidates, there is typically a need for a run-off election among the top vote-getters. It was obvious that for a Christian candidate to qualify for the run-off, he would need every vote he could get. Multiple Christian candidates would splinter the voting block, effectively excluding all of them from contention.

Though each candidate claimed to be seeking office for the good of their nation, none of them were willing to unify to ensure victory. Dr. Jean Mathurin, a Haitian friend, helped me arrange what we hopefully titled "The Haiti Christian Unity Summit." It would be held in Miami and would bring together the three presidential hopefuls along with their senior staff. It would be their first-ever, face-to-face meeting.

It began the day before Thanksgiving, 2005. Robert was not present. Before Jan and I took the flight to Miami he had shared with me his conviction that the meeting would be futile: He had absolutely no confidence that the candidates would agree to unify for the sake of their nation. I sincerely hoped he was wrong.

Inside the hotel conference room we listened as the candidates and their staff affirmed their dedication to a unified Christian government and debated how to achieve it. After an entire day of spirited discussions it was clear that there was one issue that each of the three candidates could heartily agree on: there should only be one Christian candidate for President, but each of them felt equally strongly that they should be that candidate.

Late afternoon, the following day, Jan and I flew home to Grand Rapids to celebrate what was left of the Thanksgiving holiday with our family. We left the hotel frustrated and discouraged. Despite endless hours of talking, no progress had been made. It had become clear that Robert was right.

There was no hope for political cooperation and no hope for political unity within the Christian community. None of the three politicians was willing to budge on their unshakeable commitment that he was the only Christian who should be running for office.

As it turned out, they all remained in the race and six months later, after several postponements, the election was held on February 7, 2006. The new President was René Prevál, a former associate of Bertrand Aristide, the disgraced and twice-exiled ex-president. He garnered 51.2% of the vote while Mr. Jeune, the closest Christian, came in fourth with 5.6%. For the time being, my foray into Haitian politics had come to an end.

Sometime during the summer of 2005 when my hope for a unified Christian candidacy was beginning to wane, Robert Ulysse shared with me his long-held vision for a land-development project in Northwest Haiti based on the successful Bahamian tax-free trade-zone model. He and some friends had been looking for a property they could develop into "new communities" that would bring real hope to the people of Haiti. They had settled on a 15-mile stretch of undeveloped Atlantic coastline in the northwest peninsula of Haiti near his birthplace of Jean-Rabel. As I listened to his ideas I was stunned. His vision paralleled what I had proposed to Doug Seebeck a year earlier.

On August 24, 2005 I received his business plan. The proposed mixed — use development would be known as *Nouveau Kiskeya* — a combination of French and Creole meaning "New Haiti." In early September he took some videos and prepared a DVD for me to review. A few days later, on September 8th, Jan and I agreed to provide the seed capital for the project believing it would lay the foundation for a new economy and a unique model of sustainability for Haiti.

Later that month as he was reviewing satellite images of the proposed development site something slowly dawned on Robert: incredibly, this was the exact property he had seen in a vivid dream about 23 years earlier. It had been in the early days of his marriage. Until that precise moment he'd forgotten about it completely.

I'll tell you what it really means to worship the LORD.
Remove the chains of prisoners who are chained unjustly.
Free those who are abused!
Share your food with everyone who is hungry;
share your home with the poor and homeless.
Give clothes to those in need ...
Then your light will shine in the dark;
your darkest hour will be like the noonday sun.
ISAIAH 58:6-10 (CEV)

CHAPTER 3

A Vision Is Born

AS A YOUNGSTER, ROBERT ULYSSE HAD CAUGHT THE EYE OF Baptist missionaries. He was from Jean-Rabel, an extremely poor village in Northwest Haiti. They recognized his potential and provided him with educational opportunities. Through their support he was able to attend Baptist Bible College in Springfield, Missouri. He recalls that his American friends would laugh when he pronounced the name of their state. It came out sounding like "Misery." This was not too far off; coming from the Caribbean, the mid-west winters were almost more than he could bear. He managed to stick it out and in 1983 returned to his homeland with a degree in theology and a desire to help the churches in the area where he grew up.

The contrast with the affluence he had just left behind

made the plight of his nation even more troubling. This compelled him to full-time involvement with church-based humanitarian organizations that were working in his country.

Four years later he concluded that what he along with all the other humanitarian organizations were doing would never solve the problem. Changing his strategy completely, he became involved in politics in order to address his country's obvious structural and systemic problems. His desire to help impoverished Haitians was so strong he chose to ignore the prejudice of the Christian community against those who pursued public office.

Within a few years he was a candidate for the Senate and won the election. Since the vote count in his district was disputed, rather than create a flash point of division, he chose not to claim his seat. His colleagues in the Senate petitioned for him to be appointed the Assistant Secretary of Agriculture. He ran again in the next election but, this time, because of intervention by supporters of President Jean-Bertrand Aristide, the election was called off. In 1995 Robert returned to the U.S. for graduate studies. He completed a PhD program in International Studies at Florida International University in 2003.

His courses forced him to think deeply about what lay at the core of Haiti's political and economic woes. In 1996, eight years before I would feel a compulsion to write my letter challenging American Christians to support political and economic transformation in Haiti, Robert penned a brief essay of his own. It was entitled "The Movement for Spiritual and Socioeconomic Change in Haiti." Less a political tract than a spiritual exposé, it unmasked what for Robert and many other Haitians are the historical hidden roots of Haiti's national troubles. Although this controversial interpretation of Haiti's past is frequently rejected as myth or ignored by many of his fellow countrymen, Robert took this crucial moment in Haitian history very seriously, and does to this day.

It was on August 14, 1791 that a band of desperate African slaves in St. Dominique (the French name for the island at the time) gathered secretly in a place called *Bois Caiman* — "Cayman Woods." They were overmatched and under armed. But horrific and brutal servitude that by any estimate exceeded the American slavery system by many degrees, had driven them to desperation. To ensure the success of their revolt they made a pact with their ancestral spirits.

One of the leaders was "Zamba" Boukman, a voodoo priest with an unforgettable face and imposing stature. They sacrificed a pig, renounced the white man's God, and made a covenant to serve the gods of their African ancestors who ordained vengeance. During the ceremony, one of the priests was possessed by one of the pantheon of spirits named Ezil Dantor, whose favorite animal sacrifice was a black pig. Following the ceremony this ragged, unorganized, and untrained band of slaves attacked the French Colons and went on to defeat the strongest military force in Europe. By the time the revolt ended, five thousand of Napoleon's crack troops had died, along with 18 generals.

This spiritual help was not forgotten. From 1804, the date of national independence, these spirits have been given official recognition as Haiti's "protecting gods." Whereas the perfunctory conclusion to political speeches in the United States is "God bless America," Haitian heads of state close with "May the protecting gods of the nation continue to watch over us." In the capital there is a sculpture of a pig that commemorates that water-shed event in the humid darkness of Cayman Woods.

Robert's essay urged Christians to concede that their country's social and economic troubles could be traced directly back to this Satanic pact. It boldly declared that it was time "to move from Cayman Wood to Calvary Wood." It proposed a solution to Haiti's problems: reject the passivity inherent in voodoo and unite to elect Christian leaders who would turn the nation away from its commitment to wicked spirits.

The clarity and simplicity of this call to action brought Robert to the attention of some individuals with powerful connections. They contacted him and promised him their backing for a run at the presidency in the 2000 elections. Robert agreed and assured them that the time was ripe for Haitian Christians to unite behind the candidacy of a Christian leader.

As the foundation for a grass roots movement of Christian voters was beginning, and as the momentum was building, another Christian politician, Luc Mesadieu, preempted the ground-swell by nationally publicizing that "God has chosen me to be the next president." Though this effectively destroyed the hope for a Christian coalition in time for the elections scheduled for the year 2000, Robert spent two years trying to salvage it. When it became obvious that there would be no unity, despite the emphatic disagreement of his backers, he gave up plans to launch a campaign.

This only motivated Robert to ponder his country's troubles more deeply. In 2000 he published *Plan de Liberation Economique et Sociale D'Haiti*, "Plan for the Economic and Social Liberation of Haiti." It was an amplification of his 1996 essay and proposed the formation of new rural communities that would bring about real economic development in the areas of greatest need.

Four years later, in February 2004, the country suffered its 37th coup. President Aristide, a Catholic priest, was forced out of office due to widespread allegations of corruption and brutality. Boniface Alexandre became the interim President and Gerard LaTortue, Robert's friend, was appointed Prime Minister. LaTortue asked Robert to join his cabinet as "minister without portfolio," a position which effectively made him the right-hand man of the Prime Minister.

These two friends had engaged in long and excited discussions about the creation of "new communities" that would bring economic hope to the desperately poor majority. Such was Mr. Latortue's commitment to the vision that, prior to his appointment, he had enthusiastically endorsed a project that would have involved every sector of Haitian society to bring economic development to the whole nation.

Within a few weeks of assuming the office of Prime Minister, Robert's friend had broken all his promises. His justification was the same one used by politicians the world over — the realities and complexity of the issues make idealistic dreams untenable. In a meeting in the Prime Minister's office, he explained to Robert that what he thought could be accomplished before coming to power and what could *really* be done were two entirely different things. He now claimed that their well-intentioned plans were "politically unrealistic and just not feasible." The implication was clear: belief in Haiti's radical transformation was nothing more than shallow, uninformed, naiveté.

Robert was stunned. Barely able to contain his disappointment, he looked at his friend and with deep emotion said, "Gerard, you have heard me say that Haiti is under a curse, and you have agreed." The Prime Minister looked at him intently. "However," Robert continued, "I never had any proof." Mr. Latortue shifted in his chair a bit uncomfortably, but said nothing. "Now I do."

Latortue's expression became quizzical. "What do you mean?"

"Think about what we agreed to do — what we were both committed to, and now you have put it aside completely." Latortue's face was now an inscrutable mask. "I have no other way to explain it but that you have been blinded," Robert concluded.

The two looked into each other's eyes. There was no response from Mr. Latortue. Shortly thereafter Robert tendered his resignation. He had been the Prime Minister's second-in-command for less than four months.

It was in late 2004, less than six months after Robert's resignation, that I wrote my letter to Doug Seebeck and came to Haiti to promote what I thought was a radical vision for Christian engagement in politics. I had no idea that a Haitian had preceded me with an almost identical vision. It was a few months later that he and I met at that meeting in Palm Beach with Mr. Rich DeVos.

But I was not the only one in for a surprise. Robert was moving ahead with his vision of establishing a new community near his hometown, unaware that his selection of the 15-mile stretch of oceanfront had been made for him decades earlier.

Twenty years before Robert and I met, he had a perplexing and somewhat ominous dream. He had just married Rose. They were living in Northwest Haiti near where they had both been born. Robert was working in the area as an evangelist. They had not been there very long when he had a dream that seemed to him to be more like a vision.

This is how he would later describe it to me, relating it to me as if it had occurred the night before:

> "I am in front of a Baptist church on a road that leads from Port de Paix to the town of Jean-Rabel, a distance of 44 kilometers. The road runs parallel to a large tract of coastland that has never been populated or developed. I am standing with my back to it. I am surprised to see two white men coming down toward me from the sky. They are not angels. When they descend they land on a grey material."

He explains that it is similar to cloth used in Haiti to make bags to hold money.

> "I ask them if they can give me information about the future of my wife and family.

'We have come to talk to you,' one of them states.

'I'm listening,' I respond.

The same white man says to me, 'we have come to tell you that we have great things in store for you — if you are ready.'

The word 'ready' leaps out to me. I know it is very important.

As I am thinking about what his words mean both men are lifted away and are folded up into a sky that closes behind them."

Robert woke up frightened and shared this troubling dream with his young bride. Neither could make anything out of it. He kept it to himself for several years. As time passed it melted away as strange visions usually do. It is only after a white Dutch businessman from Michigan agreed to help finance the development of a narrow strip of coastline that it occurs to him: the property at his back in his dream 20 years earlier is the same land he and I agreed to develop.

CHAPTER 4

A Passive Investment
in a God Project

BEFORE AGREEING TO INVEST IN ROBERT'S LAND-DEVELOP-
ment project I did a little investigating. The deciding factor
came when Pastor Sam, a trusted Haitian friend living in the
Fort Lauderdale area, vouched for Robert: "I can prove to
you that he is a man of integrity," he told me with a broad
smile. "How so?" I asked. Eyes gleaming with mischief he
responded, "Robert was in the government and he is still
poor." It is humorous, but then, not so funny.

My last reservation had to do with our target market.
After all, why bother building houses if there are no buy-
ers who can afford them? "Who will want to vacation or
buy property in Haiti?" I asked Robert. Since he had been
thinking about this project for several years, he responded

immediately. "Our target will be the Haitian Diaspora; the 2,000,000 Haitians living in the U.S., Canada, and France. These are the people who left Haiti during the dictator years of the 60's, 70's and early 80's. There are hundreds of thousands in the Diaspora that are reaching retirement age, and they all want to return to their homeland." I was convinced. Jan and I put in the seed money to get the project started. I believed, naively, as it turned out, that I would be an interested but passive investor.

The goal would be the creation of an attractive, stable community that would draw the Haitian "diaspora" like a magnet. And with them would come their capital and commercial expertise from years of living abroad. The first residential phase would include thousands of homes, and on the coves at each end of the property, resort communities would draw in tourist money. Thus would be birthed an economic hub that would create thousands of jobs, bless the entire region, and be replicated throughout the nation.

Robert waited to tell me that in the very center of the 15-mile property there was a strip of land several kilometers long which has been used for generations as a local curse word: *chaye* ("shayei"). It is a section of rocky coast that falls off into the Atlantic Ocean; a 50-foot drop. Haitians on the other side of the ridge that runs along the coast would threaten their children with it: "If you keep hitting your little sister I will drag you to *chaye*." Or, when anger had reached fever pitch: "Go to *chaye*!" It implies abandonment, exclusion — the place for those who are cut off from the community. Loosely translated, in this part of Haiti, *chaye* refers to Hell.

This should have served as another warning, but optimistic entrepreneur that I am, I missed its significance entirely. I also missed another important lesson. In Haiti information is parceled out with great care. If I wanted to know something I would need to ask for it. If I didn't ask, more likely than not, I would never know about it. If I didn't know what to ask for — well, that's the breaks.

Despite his reticence about *chaye,* Robert was forthcoming about the storied history of Port-a-l'Ecu, a stunning bay on the east end of the fifteen-mile property. He excitedly related how a famous explorer had stayed in that bay for 8 days in 1492. He had kept a log of his travels in which he described his lengthy voyage from Spain.

The explorer had docked first at a harbor he named Mole St. Nicholas at the western tip of Haiti's Northwest peninsula. At dawn he wanted to see more so he left early on the 6th of December heading east. Around one o'clock in the afternoon he saw a storm approaching so he began looking for a shelter for his boat and his crew. That is when he discovered this quiet bay with two rivers meandering down the slope of a small mountain on its eastern arm. The sailors threw out the anchor and began paddling to shore. Before making the beach they were startled by flying fish that kept jumping out of the water and into their boat. They were mullets.

Upon landing, the intrepid Portuguese sailor named the harbor *La Concepción.* He marched to the top of the mountain, erected a cross and claimed the island for Spain. For several centuries the island would be known by the name Hispaniola.

The explorer was an unknown Portuguese adventurer named Christopher Columbus and not many weeks later he would make the discovery that would earn him international fame. Robert assured me that while historians have chosen another bay several kilometers away as Columbus's refuge, Port-a-l'Ecu is the only bay with two rivers flowing into it. He also says that if you are paddling across the bay, mullets will still occasionally flop into your boat.

After visiting the property in November, 2005, I shared Robert's excitement and agreed with his assessment. With its stunning view of the ocean, the rugged coastline and beautiful, pristine aquamarine coves, this was well-situated land with tremendous potential. I could almost see the houses filled with people, businesses flourishing, and tourists being off-loaded from mammoth cruise liners. But more than that, what I envisioned were thousands of formerly unemployed Haitians proudly at work supporting themselves and their families.

I realized that there would be significant hurdles to getting the Nouveau Kiskeya project off the ground. I was prepared for obstacles. I expected them. As it happened, things turned out much better than I had anticipated — at least for the first few years.

At every level and at every crucial moment we were met with such favor and encouragement that my earlier assessment that this was a God-project was constantly validated. The interventions were so astonishing that I began writing them down. I called it the Miracle List. In a little over two years there would be 16 specific instances that I could only label as "miraculous." Such was their cumulative impact that I boldly began referring to Nouveau Kiskeya as a "God-project."

The first thing Robert did was to form a Haitian company known as Société Générale de Dévelopement S.A., SOGEDEV for short. He also moved his family to Port-de-Paix, the department seat in the Northwest, so he could work with the local government officials to obtain title to the roughly 11,000 acres. Port-de-Paix was only 15 kilometers away from the property, but given the condition of the roads, it required a drive of one to two hours depending on the condition of the road and how recently it had rained. He had warned me that it would take us at least a year and perhaps more to work out a land acquisition arrangement with the government. This is where the list of miracles would begin. To our shock, verbal approval was obtained within three months and a written agreement three months after that.

I was somewhat concerned that instead of a land deed our "ownership" rights were conveyed via a lease document. However, I was assured that this was standard operating practice in Haiti and that there was no need to worry since it was a "lease in perpetuity". In any event it could be converted into deeded ownership in five years. It would take me almost two years to discover the very painful lesson that our "property rights" were nowhere near as firm as I had been led to believe. Nonetheless, the speed with which these rights were obtained, given the Haitian context, was extraordinary.

To assess interest in the residential component of the project, Robert got the word out to Haitians in the Diaspora about the opportunity for them to return to Haiti and build a home on the Nouveau Kiskeya property. In less than six months over 250 expatriates demonstrated serious interest in living out their retirement years in a safe community on the island of their birth. This proved the viability of Robert's marketing theory. The immediate and extremely positive response from our "target market" again seemed to indicate that God was confirming our vision.

But we were convinced that we needed more than Haitian money and that North American investors would be essential. Finding them was to be my task. This disproved my original optimistic assumption that I would just be a passive partner.

Fortunately, I did not have to make a single "cold-call." To a man, each of the 18 American investors were referred to me. This was a huge relief since I am no fund-raiser and never wanted to be one. Before investing, however, they would invariably ask one question: "How risky is it?" My response was always the same: "If you look at the volatility of the government and the pervasive corruption in Haiti — on a purely human scale — the investment is as risky as it gets." After letting that sink in for a moment I would add, "However, if God is in it, there is no risk."

Seven investors joined us within a few months, and soon thereafter there were 18 who were willing to risk significant amounts of money with virtually no assurance of a financial return. They were compelled by the opportunity not of turning a profit but of creating thousands of jobs in the poorest country in our hemisphere. From September 2005 through January 2008 we would raise $4,000,000.

In February 2006 we faced our first financial crisis.

$60,000 was needed in ten days to pay for the property survey upon which the final acquisition of the Nouveau Kiskeya property depended. During my prayer time I told God that I considered this another "Gideon fleece." If the money was obtained, He wanted us to continue. If it was not, we were to call a halt.

On February 21, I sent an email to six prospective investors sharing our need to raise $200,000 in the next three months. I received a response from one of them that same day. It was only one sentence: "Hold $100,000 for me." Two days later another investor committed to the same amount — $200,000 in three days! What else could I conclude? God had given us His blessing to move forward.

This was my journal entry for February 28, 2006: "Lord help me to trust you for the future of Nouveau Kiskeya. (If God isn't in it, it won't work anyway.) Nouveau Kiskeya is a God project. That's the only reason I'm involved."

Within a short period it had become apparent that Robert and I did not have the expertise to manage a project of this magnitude. After all, we were envisioning an 11,000 acre residential/commercial/tourist, ocean-front development in a corner of Haiti almost completely devoid of infrastructure. Neither of us had any background for that. The only building I had done was observing my wife oversee the construction of our home. We needed very specialized, skilled help. And we needed it quickly.

I asked God to bring us the right people with the right resources at the right time. And that is exactly what happened. Through Partners Worldwide I was introduced to

Steve Westra who had owned a large construction company in Wisconsin. He introduced me to his friend Rob Petroelje who had founded V3 Companies, Ltd., a prestigious Chicago engineering firm.

Several months later I received a call from Dave Arnold. He had heard about our Haitian project through a friend of a friend. He introduced himself and shared that he had been in the process of starting an international land-development company to do construction and land-development work in the Caribbean. Dave and I met the following week in South Bend, Indiana. Not long after that Dave began to play an integral role in the development of Nouveau Kiskeya.

As God was providing the money and these technical experts to guide the project, it was becoming increasingly apparent that it was time to organize the investors into an official organization. I invited the first seven investors to a meeting in Chicago. I offered to be responsible for its ongoing oversight if they would agree to serve as a board. They agreed and within hours we set up plans to form the SOGEDEV Equity Group LLC., (SEG). A few months later we hired the company Dave Arnold and Rob Petroelje had formed to be the project manager.

Later that same year our backs were once again up against the wall. On November 13, 2006 we were down to $10,000 in our bank account. This was insufficient for us to make the month-end payroll. But I was convinced God had blessed our venture and did not feel the slightest anxiety. In my phone conversation with Dave Arnold I told Dave, "I wonder how God will work this one out?"

The following day I received a call from a prospective investor who had called me out of the blue several weeks before. He wanted to meet for breakfast the next morning. I left that meeting with a commitment for $100,000. The next day at our monthly SEG Board meeting the members pledged another $110,000. In three days $210,000 had been raised without even needing to prime the pump. My confidence in God's sponsorship of the vision soared, yet there were constant, serious challenges.

A journal entry from around that time reflects how I was responding to these difficulties that kept forcing us to ask whether we should go forward or stop? I wrote, "I am ready to move forward in faith because I believe *God will provide* as He has so many times before on this project. I am curious, though, how He will provide. I also wonder if God is using this process to draw us closer to Himself. I think that is true for me. I think I am getting better at trusting that God will provide ... Thank you Jesus that I am finally beginning to not only believe that, but to live it. It's been a long journey from knowing STOP (Surrender, Trust, Obey, Praise) to living STOP. I'm not there yet but I'm getting closer."

> *And what does the LORD require of you?*
> *To act justly and to love mercy*
> *and to walk humbly with your God.*
> MICAH 6:8

CHAPTER 5

A Miracle Well, a Conversion and Our First Prime Minister

IN ADDITION TO MONEY, ALL DEVELOPMENT PROJECTS NEED water. This is particularly important in countries where fresh drinking water is scarce. That was certainly the case at Nouveau Kiskeya. But what made matters much more discouraging was the long-standing opinion of Haitian experts that drilling in Northwest Haiti was a waste of time. Despite these negative reports, we still decided to move ahead. We did not know that our search for a supposedly non-existent resource would result not only in a spectacular discovery but an even more dramatic conversion.

In early 2007 we hired hydro-geologists from V3, Rob Petroelje's company, to find this precious commodity. They scoured international geological records to determine the best possible location for drilling. After an exhaustive three-month investigation that included crawling around thousands of acres, James Adamson and Stuart Dykstra, our two hydro-geologists, finally settled on a site twelve kilometers inland from our property. It was on the shoulder of what is known as Bamboo Mountain and was owned by Innocent Duclos, a 70-year-old farmer.

Robert negotiated the deal with Innocent's son-in-law sitting in the pasture under a tree. A few of the locals observed the formal proceedings while clustered a respectful 100 feet away. After nearly an hour of conversation, the topic of purchasing the land was finally brought up. Eventually a deal was struck for 1.2 acres at a cost of $1,500. It was a very favorable price for the seller. To avoid any possible contentious arguments later on we wanted to make sure that Innocent was completely pleased with the agreement.

A one-kilometer road had to be built to the drilling site. When it was completed, it took three days to get the rig in place. We were told that the shaft of the drilling rig could not exceed 320 feet, the maximum extension of the drill stem. Every day a curious and excited group numbering 50 to 100 people crowded around the drillers. Enterprising women set up vending "shops" where they sold coffee, fried bananas, bread and spicy peanut brittle.

After three days of drilling, on May 14, 2007, the drill point hit the aquifer. The crowd erupted. Women danced and everyone began clapping and chanting in Creole. We had found a "gusher." It was a well capable of producing one million gallons of fresh potable water per day! The shaft was 318 feet deep. Had the aquifer been three feet deeper we might have missed it. This was one more entry for the Miracle List; another affirmation that this was a God-project.

What none of us knew was that Innocent, the owner of the land, had spent 15 years seeking deliverance from what he believed was a severe voodoo spell over his life. He consulted as many voodoo priests as he could. Each one gave him different charms to cling to for deliverance — nothing worked. When water was struck by this group who had a different God than he did, hope began to rise in his heart. He was also astonished that the "blancs", rather than taking advantage of the water to make a huge profit, were giving it away for free. Innocent kept his eye on them for months and began wondering if it had been their God who had sent these people to his land.

It was the commemorative service we held at the well that convinced him. In November 2007, Jan and I, joined by several of the Nouveau Kiskeya investors, travelled to the well site for a celebration and dedication ceremony. When we arrived, a large group of Haitians was already waiting for us. Many of them belonged to a nearby Christian church. We interacted with them as best we could despite the language barrier. Virtually none of them spoke English and most of us did not speak Creole, so we decided to sing some well-known Christian hymns. The locals sang in Creole and the Americans in English. It was an unusually moving occasion.

Caught up in the celebration, I was unaware that Innocent had joined the crowd gathered around the well. While we were singing he had quietly made his way over and was watching all of us with keen interest. As we were preparing to leave, he approached Robert and whispered, "We have to talk."

They met several days later and continued to meet for the next several months. Innocent asked Robert for his help in freeing him from the grip of voodoo. On a Monday afternoon in March a group of Christians from the nearby village of Café-Paul, accompanied by Robert and some of our Christian employees, went to Innocent's house. After an extended time of joyful praise interspersed with powerful prayers from his Christian neighbors, Innocent was led to confess his sins and accept Jesus as his Savior.

Following his confession of faith the group combed through his very modest home and removed every voodoo-related item. Marching and singing a victory song, the band of Christians carried these articles, including the "sacred" table used for ritual sacrifice, and threw them onto a large pile. A bonfire was set and soon everything was consumed.

The news of Innocent's conversion circulated around the nearby villages. An even greater interest was stirred when he offered his house to be used as a church for his new God. That following Sunday, the first service was held in Innocent's house. Eight months after the date of his conversion, on November 28, 2008, Innocent Duclos left this earth to meet his Savior.

God's blessing continued unabated, but after two years I was finding the peaks and valleys emotionally exhausting. In June of 2007 I wrote in my journal, "I need to surrender the concern about raising money. My job is simply to be available and pray 'show me Lord what it is You want me to do' (Psalm 143:10) and God will do the rest."

Nouveau Kiskeya had been started with a triple-bottom line: job creation, spiritual impact and profitability to assure viability. But I was aware, even then, that spiritual focus could easily be eclipsed by the other priorities that clamored for attention on a project of this size; especially raising money. Another journal entry that month indicated my primary commitment, at least on an intellectual level: "The only thing that the people of Haiti need more than jobs is a restored relationship with the God of the Bible. That is why we need to be about the work of Spiritual transformation using business as the platform." This was a noble goal but it would prove to be very elusive.

The following month I wrote something that several years later would prove eerily prophetic: "We need the power of the Kingdom of God to fight the power of the Kingdom of darkness. This is especially true in Haiti. Only divine power can conquer the demonic power that rules Haiti." I did not know that voodoo and demons would one day become much more than a nebulous religious concept for me.

In July 2007, two months after finding water, we received an invitation to meet with the Haitian Prime Minister, Jacques Édouard Alexis and his cabinet. Mr. Alexis was a dominating, affable politician with a good grasp of English. He was clearly the most powerful man in the room. At the time I was not fully aware that a Haitian Prime Minister's position can be very tenuous and that his or her authority can vanish quickly at the whim of the Legislature or that of the President.

Though constitutional reforms have raised the authority of the Prime Minster above that of President (to counteract almost 200 years of dictatorial abuse by office-holders who appointed themselves president-for-life), political reality has yet to catch up. It wasn't until much later that we began to understand that the Haitian President still usually trumps the Prime Minister.

Alexis was decisive and made it clear to us that he was intrigued by the potential of our project. We were encouraged that we had such a strong ally in high places. Unfortunately, and to our surprise, the President allowed Prime Minister Alexis to be forced out of office nine months later as a scape-goat to appease the people who were rioting in the streets because of sharp increases in food prices.

During our meetings, Prime Minister Alexis made two statements that stand out clearly in my mind. The first was a question. After reviewing our documentation and the scope of the project he asked us: "Where have you been?" He had a broad smile, but his eyes looked at us sharply. What he was diplomatically conveying was that projects of this magnitude should have been reviewed by the national leaders long before breaking ground. We had been in business for almost two years without obtaining their sanction. Early on I had been advised that it would be best for us to keep away from the scrutiny of the politicians in Port-au-Prince. The counsel we received was that this was necessary in order to avoid demands for monumental bribes. Looking at the piercing expression on the Prime Minister's face I started to wonder whether that had been good advice.

In response to the Prime Minister's question, our Haitian attorney explained that there is nothing in Haitian law that requires a duly-registered national entity to solicit permission from national leaders before they go about their business. The Prime Minister's retort was, "That's a new way of doing things," at which point everyone in the room laughed. I didn't realize that, despite his smile, he was sending us a signal that we were embarked on a course that ran directly counter to powerful currents of long-standing practice and entrenched self-interest. That was another warning I missed.

Several of the cabinet leaders were not so subtle. The Minister of Finance and the Minister of Public Works made their opposition quite obvious. We would find out later that they were close friends of President René Préval, the man who was really calling the shots. They badgered us repeatedly with distorted and erroneous observations and sought to mire us in unproductive discussions about minor details.

They kept drawing the conversation back to a slight misspelling of the name of our Haitian corporation in the registration application. It became clear to us that they were doing everything in their power to derail the dialogue and bring a halt to any productive interaction with Prime Minister Alexis. Though I was frustrated, I failed to appreciate the seriousness of this opposition. Ultimately it would turn out to be the most significant barrier to the accomplishment of the vision I was confident God had given us.

The other statement that I vividly remember the Prime Minister making that day is: "Welcome to Haiti. Haiti is open for business!" In time I would discover to my great frustration that this was not the case. Sadly, it may have been sincere, but if it was, it was mere wishful thinking. Four years later I read in the Miami Herald that another Haitian politician, President Michel Joseph Martelly, had made the same declaration. It reminded me of Mr. Alexis and it made me a little sad. I hope it is true but, down deep, I doubt it.

Our last question to the Prime Minister was an obvious one: "Who in your government should we consider as our primary contact?" Mr. Alexis had taken notice of the opposition. He could have assigned Nouveau Kiskeya to the Minister of Finance or to the Minister of Public Works. Either of these men would have been logical choices. The Prime Minister also knew that either one of these men would immediately kill the project. But he didn't. Instead, he transferred it directly to his own office and assigned Dr. Jean Mathurin, his chief economic advisor, as our liaison.

As it happened, Dr. Mathurin was a Christian and Robert's long-time friend. Jean Mathurin and I had become friends two years earlier when we had co-sponsored the Haiti Christian Unity Summit in Miami. This sign of apparent divine favor caused us to minimize the dark clouds of resistance. We would come to see that that had been a mistake.

CHAPTER 6

I was hungry and you gave me something to eat,
I was thirsty and you gave me something to drink,
I was a stranger and you invited me in,
I needed clothes and you clothed me,
I was sick and you looked after me,
I was in prison and you came to visit me.

MATTHEW 25:35-36

Shaken to the Core

AT THE END OF 2007, ON THE BRINK OF A NEW YEAR, IT seemed as though we were poised for a major leap forward. Considering the experts' negativity, the discovery of water less than twelve kilometers from our property seemed to be another miracle. Reinforcing that positive assessment was the Prime Minister's support of our project. His decision to shield us from influential politicians intent on derailing the Nouveau Kiskeya initiative looked like just one more sign of God's favor on Nouveau Kiskeya.

Irrespective of what I had written in my journal on some of my better days, I had struggled intensely through the financial challenges we had encountered. And carrying the load of this massive project that was providing work for over a thousand Haitians had at times been exhausting. I was aware that this was way beyond my capability and capacity, but I was convinced that if it truly was a God project I had no options other than to move forward in faith.

Despite the "miracles" I continued to struggle with the question whether Nouveau Kiskeya really had divine sanction. This was my journal entry in September 2007: "Are you working on a God project or a good project? If your answer is a God project, don't worry about stuff. God will provide." This entry was followed by something I would revisit years later in the midst of a crucible that would threaten to crush me: "Either the God of the Bible exists or He doesn't. If God exists He controls the world and Nouveau Kiskeya and He loves the Haitian people and me. Therefore everything will be OK. If He doesn't exist, Nouveau Kiskeya doesn't really matter. I believe God exists."

As we celebrated the beginning of 2008 I did not know I was entering the year that would shake me to the core. Wednesday morning, the 30th day of January, I received the first of four shocks that would stretch out over four months. On that frigid Michigan morning as I entered my office, I took a telephone call I will never forget. It was from Dave Arnold, our project manager, informing me that the Nouveau Kiskeya project had been shut down by the Haitian government! That same morning I received an email confirmation from Robert in which he attached the letter from the Government. It was signed by Haiti's Director General, the equivalent of the U.S. Director of the IRS. It was titled, "Stoppage of all activities." I was stunned!

Specifically, it informed us that the General Office of

Taxes "seizes this opportunity to ask you to stop all activities on the state property occupied in Port-a-l'Ecu, Jean-Rabel, pending the signing of the proper contract with the Haitian State." Effectively, the letter was an immediate, unequivocal (and indefinite) stop-work order. We knew that it was no coincidence that the order had been issued from an office that reported directly to the Minister of Finance. No explanation was offered. Despite repeated attempts over the next twelve months to get an explanation, we would never get a clear answer to our question.

Despite the order's lack of clarity, we had no choice but to immediately terminate the more than one thousand people who had been employed building a seven-kilometer access road to the property. The local government had been thrilled at our offer to construct what could have become the best road in Northwest Haiti. In exchange for our assuming responsibility for payroll and materials, they had given us permission to use some of their heavy equipment. When the letter arrived we had been engaged in this cooperative project for several months and had completed about 70% of the roadway.

The second shock occurred less than one month later. On February 20 our American attorneys advised us to set up an escrow account in excess of one million dollars to cover potential liabilities to Haitian expatriates who had expressed an interest in Nouveau Kiskeya in early 2006. We did not have anywhere near enough to cover that potential liability.

Already reeling, we received a third shock in March that made me feel like we were getting battered by one of Haiti's famously destructive hurricanes. During a conference call updating the status of the project, one of our investors asked me if we were complying with the Foreign Corrupt Practices Act (FCPA). That was the first time I had ever heard the name. Shortly I would find out that it is a little-known but very potent American law drafted to prevent corruption by US corporations operating in foreign nations. It prohibits "an offer or payment of anything of value to government officials … to secure any improper advantage in order to obtain or retain business."

After consulting with our attorneys, I learned that the FCPA imposes severe sanctions on any US corporation that participates "knowingly or unknowingly" in bribery of government officials. It was that "unknowingly" part that caused my heart to drop. A corporation held in violation could face a possible $2,000,000 fine and its officers could be subject to incarceration. That got all of our attention. Our legal team suggested that we immediately adopt a specific anti-bribery policy and engage in a due-diligence analysis to verify that we had not inadvertently run afoul of this law.

That same day we prepared a questionnaire and sent it to Robert. We told him about the importance and urgency of the questions and asked for a response within two or three days. His answers arrived in less than 24-hours. Unfortunately, his answers were not encouraging. He informed us, without the slightest reticence, that at least nine "courtesy gifts" (which he explained were simply standard protocol in dealing with government officials) had been offered over the past two years.

When I read Robert's response I felt numb; this violation of American law could threaten our very survival.

As if this was not enough, the forth shock arrived three weeks later. It was April 12, 2008. Prime Minister Alexis, who in July 2007 had assured us that "Haiti was open for business," lost a "no-confidence" vote in the Haitian Senate. This meant that he immediately lost his job as Prime Minister. For us that meant that our most important political ally was gone. Not only had we lost a friend in high places, but also, without a Prime Minister, Haiti no longer had a functioning government.

According to the Haitian constitution, when a Prime Minister is dismissed in this manner the entire Cabinet is also terminated. As a result, all government activities, other than those that are absolutely crucial to keep the country operational, are put on hold until the House of Deputies and the Senate confirms a new Prime Minister and a new Cabinet.

Since we were still operating under a "stop-work" order we were essentially paralyzed. There was no official to whom we could address our questions or request a resolution of this stalemate. In the end it would take three candidates, four hurricanes, and five months of agonizing delays before the Haitian Government would begin to function again under the leadership of a new Prime Minister: Madam Michelle Pierre-Louis.

Given the shocking events of the first four months of 2008, our management team spent the month of May evaluating options. We concluded that trying to raise investment money under these adverse conditions was inadvisable and probably impossible. However, it was also obvious that, unless some drastic action was taken, we would run out of money. By the end of the month we had agreed to "mothball" the project. Unfortunately this meant terminating our relationship with management team members Dave Arnold and Rob Petroelje and eliminating all positions at Nouveau Kiskeya other than a minimal maintenance and security staff.

During that summer there was nothing we could do to get the project back on track. The leadership vacuum in the Haitian Government had not been filled and there was no one, except the President, from whom we could seek an explanation or recourse. Efforts to meet with him brokered by a mysterious Catholic priest were not successful.

During the next five months the President nominated three candidates for Prime Minister. The first two were rejected by the legislature. Finally, the third, Madam Pierre-Louis, was confirmed on September 5, 2008. To this day, I am convinced that the reason Madam Pierre-Louis was hastily confirmed was because four hurricanes in as many weeks had resulted in significant loss of life in Haiti and the International Community was unwilling to respond with assistance until a new government was formed.

With the new leadership in place we reinitiated attempts to meet with high-level government officials. Several weeks later we were invited to Port-au-Prince to meet with our nemesis, the Minister of Finance, and the new Prime Minister's Chief of Staff. We were disappointed to find out that despite the change in government the Minister of Finance had been reappointed. But there was a glimmer of hope in the midst of the rolling thunderclouds. Madame Pierre-Louis had also selected our good friend Dr. Jean Mathurin as her Chief Economic Advisor. I clung to the hope that God was still orchestrating events to resolve the immovable roadblocks that seemed to be piling up in our path.

Less than three weeks later Dave Arnold and I were at the Finance Ministers office in Port-au-Prince. True to form, the Minister kept us waiting for almost an hour. It was a transparent attempt to emphasize his power over us. I wondered whether Moses and Aaron had received the same treatment from the Egyptian Pharaoh.

The Minister invited five of his staff members to join us. The first half of the two-hour meeting was consumed by his rambling and confusing explanation of the basis for shutting down the Nouveau Kiskeya project. He made a major point of the fact that it was his job to protect the interests of the Haitian people. I thought, but did not say that as Minister of Finance, I would have assumed that creating jobs for the Haitian people would also be high on his list of priorities. As I listened to his incoherent monologue, I doubted that jobs were anywhere on his priority list. When he had finished, I asked the question for which we had been desperately seeking an answer for nine months: "What do we need to do to get the 'stop-work' order lifted?" I was shocked by his answer: "All that is required is for you to put your request in writing." I refrained from asking him why he had not told us this 9 months earlier when we had repeatedly asked his office this same question.

In addition, he wanted us to submit multiple copies of

our business plan to the Ministry of Finance so that it could be "distributed among the appropriate officials." Again I restrained myself. We submitted to this most classic of bureaucratic demands, even though we had sent multiple copies of this very plan to various government offices, including the Office of the Ministry of Finance, several times during the prior twelve months.

Towards the end of the meeting, the Minister of Finance made a show of reinforcing his understanding of business, and his awareness that "in business time is money." As proof of his sensitivity to this issue he requested that we clearly communicate our timelines so that his office could respond to us on a timely basis. He appointed his Chief of Staff as our chief liaison to his office. All indications from this meeting were that both sides appeared to be interested in starting over and working towards a Public Private Partnership between the Haitian government and the Nouveau Kiskeya project.

Within one week we had once again sent everything the Minister of Finance had requested via overnight mail. We received no acknowledgement. Our repeated telephone calls over the next 30 days to the Chief of Staff were not answered. The Ministry of Finance had gone silent.

The SEG Board, representing the American investors, had been scheduled to meet on the afternoon of October 28, 2008. Our main agenda item was to talk about our progress in lifting the "stop-work" order. As the date for the meeting drew near and the Finance Minister continued to ignore us, I sadly prepared a recommendation that we withdraw from the Nouveau Kiskeya project. However, my formal proposal to pull the plug was kept at bay by persistent rumors that Prime Minister Pierre-Louis was preparing to send us a letter indicating her support.

Four hours before the Board meeting the letter arrived. As we had been informed, it expressed her strong backing and her decision to set up a special task force to "process our proposal with the utmost urgency." We were somewhat skeptical because we had received three similar promises over the past two years, but we refused to be completely cynical. It was conceivable that this could be one more last-minute intervention to add to the Miracle List. After reading the letter to the Board I suggested that we postpone a final decision for 30 days. They agreed.

I sent the Prime Minister a personal note thanking her for her support and suggesting that it would be helpful if we could have a personal meeting. Over the next several weeks I corresponded with my friend, Jean Mathurin, Chief Economic Advisor to the new Prime Minister. I pressed him for a clear directive about the process for re-activating Nouveau Kiskeya.

My patience was again beginning to wear thin as I waited for a response from Jean. Finally, after waiting for almost a month, on November 25 he sent me a troubling email. He expressed his confusion about our insistence on the lifting of the "stop-work" order and essentially set that issue aside. Instead he asked for the submission of detailed information about our development plan and the financial capacity of our investors. His explanation was that he and the Prime Minister "needed it to combat opposition within various sectors of the government." He went on to say: "This data is necessary to enrich our arguments in order to be able to pass over the traditional views and fears of our authorities towards foreign investors."

That final sentence confirmed my worst fears. The inexplicable delays and mixed-messages we'd received had caused me to begin to suspect that there was something more serious behind the opposition than mere bureaucratic bungling and internal turf-wars. I had been slowly coming to the conclusion that at its core lay a culturally entrenched, deep-seated fear of foreign intervention. The island nation's sordid history of occupation and slavery seemed to have embedded within the Haitian psyche a reactionary posture of suspicion, especially of "blancs" intent on gaining "ownership rights" over their land. As a result, despite what we had been assured, Haiti was not really open for business after all.

Something else was becoming abundantly clear: the current Prime Minister lacked the political strength to overrule the Finance Minister even though he was a member of her Cabinet. Later we would be made aware that President Preval and the Minister of Finance were long-time friends. We were again reminded that regardless of its Constitution, nothing much happens in Haiti without the President's approval.

Because of Thanksgiving holiday travel, I did not respond to Jean's email until December 5, 2008. My response was an uncharacteristically lengthy four-page letter, which I addressed to Prime Minister Madame Pierre-Louis and asked Jean to deliver for me. In it I carefully explained the frustration of the American investors who were primarily interested in creating jobs in her country. Our position was simple: if steps were not taken to remove the road-blocks to cooperation, we would have no choice but to withdraw from the project.

As the follow-up Board meeting date approached, I again prepared a recommendation to halt continued involvement in the Nouveau Kiskeya project. The Board Meeting started at 11:00 AM on December 23, 2008. Once more I heard rumors that another letter was on its way from the Prime Minister. I kept an eye on my email in-box while chairing the Board Meeting. Thirteen minutes into the meeting it arrived. I asked Dave Arnold to read it to the Board members.

The prime Minister acknowledged my four-page letter and conveyed the following sentiment: *"I appreciate the openness of your response and I understand your concerns regarding the time it is taking to process this dossier. My wish is that this project and all the others that have a similar scope receive a special treatment."*

Her letter concluded with a personal invitation to meet with her and some of her Cabinet Members on January 29, 2009 at her office in Port-au-Prince. Again, as a Board, we concluded that we had no choice. We were meeting to consider terminating our involvement in the Nouveau Kiskeya project and at the eleventh hour it appeared that God had again cracked open a door.

In retrospect I still do not think it was unreasonable for us to assume that this was God's hand at work beckoning us to move forward in faith. We agreed that we should exercise patience, trust Him, walk through this opening and see what lay on the other side. My journal entry for the end of 2008 reflects a major change in my once unshakable assumption that a God-project would inevitably succeed:

> *"Just because you are doing what God wants you to do,*
> *does not necessarily mean you will get*
> *the results you are expecting."*

We do not know what to do
but our eyes are on you.
II CHRONICLES 20:12B

CHAPTER 7

The Day God Went Silent

OUR "MAKE-IT OR BREAK-IT" MEETING WITH PRIME MINIS-
ter Madam Pierre-Louis was scheduled for 11:00 a.m., Thursday, January 29, 2009. It had not escaped me that this was
exactly 365 days from the date we had received the stop-work
order that had completely shut down our project.

The events of the past year had made me increasingly
aware that we were facing serious opposition. And with it
had come the realization that we had enemies in the same
sense that King David had enemies. I had been in business
in the United States for 40 years, yet I don't believe that in all
that time I had ever had an enemy. But now I was operating
in a different world. Not only did we have people who were
directly opposed to us but many of them sat in government
offices in Port-au-Prince.

I discussed these observations with some friends. They suggested that I might very well be involved in a spiritual battle. At the time I did not know much about what that meant. I had read the *Left Behind* series but had concluded that this kind of battle took place somewhere in the "sky" between angels and demons. I was unaware that it can take place right here and can involve human beings who are directly, though perhaps unconsciously, involved in a war between good and evil. I had not taken seriously what the Bible teaches about the nature of the battle Christians face in this world. As a result I didn't appreciate the very real influence demons can have on such issues as depression, discouragement and distraction, just to name a few. I could relate to all three.

As a result of this lack of understanding, I made multiple tactical and strategic errors. I did not know that I had been deceived. I had concluded, quite naturally, that what we were facing was simply a human struggle against ignorance, jealousy or greed and nothing more. As a result I was operating exclusively on the battlefield of logic and persuasion not realizing that the opposition had a completely different set of tools and a completely different end-goal in mind. I came to see this later when it was almost too late.

As we prepared for the meeting with the Prime Minister we were made aware that the resistance from the Minister of Finance was actually increasing. Jean Mathurin, our primary contact person, had alerted us to the suspicions and rumors that were beginning to circulate throughout the government. It was not difficult to guess which office was behind them.

Questions were being raised for the first time about

our financial capacity as well as our technical competence to pull off a project of this magnitude. This prompted us to put together a select team of seven people for this high-level meeting with the Prime Minister. Three members of our team were representatives of Panorama International, a firm with 40 years of experience in large-scale land development projects in 70 countries.

In our communications with Jean Mathurin we had agreed that the mutually-desired outcome of the meeting would be the issuance of a Memorandum of Understanding or "Accord Cadre" as it is referred to in Haiti. The Accord would be simple. It would specify that the Government of Haiti and the Nouveau Kiskeya project had agreed to work in good faith toward a Public Private Partnership for the benefit of the Haitian people. In essence, it was a formal agreement to cooperate on writing a more detailed formal cooperation agreement later. It was an official agreement to reach an agreement.

In addition to working out a draft version of the Accord Cadre, Jean had also agreed to our request for a preliminary meeting with senior ministerial staff. He concurred that this would ensure maximum efficiency, as it would give both sides an opportunity to address any concerns, questions or misunderstandings before the official gathering.

Jean made the arrangements and assured us that we could meet with the senior staff at 1:00 PM on Wednesday, the day prior to our meeting with the Prime Minister and her Cabinet. He informed us that he had made sure that the draft of the proposed Accord had been circulated among the principals. We expressed our appreciation for his help and he assured us enthusiastically that, other than minor modifications, we should plan to leave the Prime Minister's office with a signed version of the Accord Cadre. For the first time in a long while, I felt my hope and confidence index begin to rise.

Our development team arrived in Port-au-Prince on Tuesday the 27th with great expectations. That evening Jean met us on the deck of the Montana Hotel to go over some final arrangements. During our conversation, he nonchalantly mentioned that our Wednesday meeting with the ministerial staff had been cancelled. When we asked why, his response was, "It is not necessary." We were stunned!

He hurriedly assured us that since there was broad approval on the language, everything could be handled at the meeting with the Prime Minister. He reiterated his guarantee that the Accord Cadre would be signed at the conclusion of the meeting.

At 7:00 AM on the morning of the big meeting, I received a phone call in my hotel room. It was from Jean. He was calling to relay the details of the day's schedule. It was the most detailed agenda I had ever been given. I was encouraged by its precision since it seemed to indicate that the Prime Minister was treating this meeting with unique care and concern.

We were to arrive at her office by 10:45 AM and would be escorted to her Conference Room so that we would be ready for her entrance into the room at 10:59. Upon entering she would greet each of the participants and make her introductory remarks. This would run from 11:03 until 11:18. At that point I would be given the floor and allowed nine minutes for my introduction. Then, at 11:27, discussion would begin. Our meeting would conclude at precisely 1:00 PM.

Our delegation arrived at the Prime Minister's office at 10:30 AM, fifteen minutes early. We were escorted to a waiting area. We took our seats and remained there for a full hour. At 11:30 AM we were escorted to the Conference Room and told that the start time had been delayed because one of the Ministers "is still on his way." As it turned out, the official who was "unavoidably" delayed was our nemesis, the Minister of Finance. While we waited for him the Prime Minister, Madam Pierre-Louis, entered the conference room. She greeted each of us then made her way back to her private chambers.

At 12:00 noon the Minister of Finance arrived, precisely one hour late. The Prime Minister re-entered the room, took her seat at the head of the table, and made her formal introductory remarks. I then spoke briefly. I explained that we were a group of Christian businessmen who were motivated by our faith to create jobs for the Haitian people. I introduced the members of our team and explained that our goal was to work toward the creation of a private public partnership with the Haitian Government. I emphasized our hope that we could agree to partner together for the benefit of both parties but, most importantly, for the benefit of the Haitian people.

The Prime Minister then opened the meeting to questions and discussion. Within a few minutes two heated conversations had broken out, one in English and the other in French. The reason for the competing languages was that several of the Ministers neither spoke nor understood English. What was infuriating to me was that when we inquired about the need for an interpreter several days earlier we had been assured that would be unnecessary since everyone present was fluent in English. This was clearly not the case. In addition, it was soon apparent that the Prime Minister had lost control of the meeting.

From what I could understand, several of the Ministers were insisting that the government lacked sufficient information about the Nouveau Kiskeya project to sign even a preliminary agreement. This was of course ludicrous since we had sent multiple copies of the project dossiers, on several occasions, to various government offices during the past sixteen months.

What was even more frustrating to us was that this purported insufficiency of information could have easily been corrected had the officials followed through on our agreement for a preliminary meeting. As I quietly seethed, it dawned on me that in reality, this would not have made the slightest difference. Had that issue been resolved another would have been raised as an insurmountable obstacle.

The body posture of the Minister of Finance said it all. Throughout the meeting, he sat back in his chair with his arms folded, a closed portfolio in front of him. When he finally opened his mouth it was only to ask the same questions he had raised in our meeting with Prime Minister Alexis a year-and-a-half earlier. Each of his questions had been answered repeatedly and all of the documentation he had requested had been sent — in triplicate. He was only making a point: *I am completely opposed to your project and nothing you say is going to change my mind.*

It did not take us very long to realize that, contrary to what we had been told, there would be no Accord Cadre signed that day — and most likely not on any other day. Madame Louis Pierre apparently came to the same conclusion, wrapped up the meeting, thanked us for coming, and told us that we could expect to receive official written notification of the government's position on our project shortly.

Since some of our team had flights back to Miami that afternoon, we had just enough time for a one-hour debriefing. On the patio of the Montana Hotel overlooking Port-au-Prince, our team agreed that we faced serious, high-level opposition and that there was little indication that the government was willing to cooperate with us.

One of them stated that in the best-case scenario, even if we could overcome these obstacles, it was virtually impossible to imagine partnering with the current Haitian government given the dysfunction we had just observed and the delays we had experienced over the past 18 months. We all understood the necessity of significant government support and cooperation for the success of this public/private venture. Before we left we shared our suspicion that because of the powerful forces arrayed against us, barring an act of God, our involvement in the project was probably over.

In a sense I was relieved. We had dealt with a great deal of uncertainty for over one year. My prayer had been that God would give us a clear indicator and that our team would be united in its perception of the future of the project. I was tired of the uncertainty and had wanted either a green or a red light. As far as I was concerned we had been operating under a yellow light for too long. If nothing else, following this meeting I had to admit that God had answered this prayer. It was now very clear that we were looking at a red light.

Four days later, on February 3, 2009, we held a conference call with the SEG Board. I told them that the management team had unanimously agreed that U.S. ownership and control of the Nouveau Kiskeya project could not continue and that no further funds should be raised to sustain it. I shared my reasons for these drastic recommendations. We had lost faith in the current government's capacity to enter into an international partnership. Haiti, it appeared to us, lacked government officials with sufficient courage to risk their position to make difficult decisions. Even if we could manage to obtain a partnership agreement with the government, we had no confidence in their ability to live up to it. In addition, I told them that the essential ingredients for a successful partnership between our team and the Haitian Government; common goals, common values, trust, integrity and respect, were missing. I also suggested that it might not even be possible for an American company to function ethically in Haiti's pervasive climate of corruption.

Following my explanation the Board voted to cease operations. We agreed that we would seek to transfer ownership of Nouveau Kiskeya to another investment group that would be better prepared to tread through the murky Haitian political waters. Several months later we transferred our equity in Nouveau Kiskeya to Robert Ulysse and his Haitian partners in return for a promissory note. The legal work was completed on April 30, 2009. As we signed the final triplicate set of documents, in English and in French, I felt drained. I was emotionally, spiritually and physically exhausted. I felt numb. This time there was no last-minute communication from the Prime Minister. No letter and no miracle. It seemed that both the Prime Minister's office and God had gone silent.

While we were wrapping up our involvement in Nouveau Kiskeya, I spent a great deal of time trying to make sense of what had happened. We had begun with such hope. We had committed to an ambitious project that had been driven not by greed, but by compassion. When I had prayed for specific confirmations, I had received them time and again; many in dramatic and incontrovertible ways. On at least 16 occasions we had been given what I could only conclude were miraculous affirmations to continue forward. The following is just a partial list:

1. In November 2004, I was prompted by the Spirit of God, to write a letter to Doug Seebeck, outlining my concerns that we as American Christians were only offering Band-Aids to the people in Haiti. As a result of this letter I met the following people within the next 60 days:

   - Chavannes Jeune, a Christian Pastor who was running for President of Haiti

   - Robert Ulysse, a Christian who had served at high levels of the Haitian Government

   - Mr. Richard DeVos, who agreed to help us help the people in Haiti

2. When we started the land acquisition process for Nou-veau Kiskeya, Robert indicated that this might be a 2 – 3 year process. Instead, we had verbal agreement with the Haitian Government in 3 months and a written agree-ment in 6 months.

3. In February 2006, the Nouveau Kiskeya project needed $200,000 to pay some of the costs of land acquisition. I told God that I would consider getting or not getting that money as a clear indicator of whether He was involved in this project. This money was raised within a week on the basis of a simple email.

4. During the next several years we would raise $4,000,000 from 18 investors. Each one of these investors came to me or was referred by a mutual friend. I never made a cold call to raise money.

5. As the project became more complex we needed exper-tise that Robert and I did not have. My simple prayer was "God, please bring us the right people with the right resources at the right time". As a result, God brought us Steve Westra, Rob Petroelje, Dave Arnold, Stuart Dykstra, James Adamson, Ben Eldridge, Neil Van Dine and others.

6. The Nouveau Kiskeya property was quite inaccessible when we began to work there in 2005. Part of the inacces-sibility was the result of a river, over 100 yards wide, that did not have a bridge. The water height, influenced by the amount of recent rain in the region, determined whether it was safe to drive through the river. As a result, we added an airstrip to the property design specifications. Shortly

after, on a Sunday afternoon, Robert received a call from an elderly gentleman who had grown up in the area. He wondered if Robert knew that at one time there had been an airstrip right on the Nouveau Kiskeya property! With the elderly gentleman's assistance the location of the airstrip was discovered, very overgrown but still viable.

7. Monday November 13, 2006 we were down to $10,000 in our bank account. We were looking at a payroll that would consume all of that and more. The very next day I received a call from a potential investor indicating that he was ready to meet. He committed to investing $100,000. That same week the Board Members agreed to invest another $110,000.

8. The miraculous story about how we found a one million gallon per day water source for Nouveau Kiskeya is told in a prior chapter.

9. Despite all of our struggles with Haitian Government leaders, our friend, Dr. Jean Mathurin was consistently appointed and reappointed as our chief liaison with the government.

10. In November, 2008 some of our Board members and I visited the Nouveau Kiskeya project. Robert asked us to join him as he made a courtesy call on the mayor of Jean-Rabel, a city located near the Nouveau Kiskeya property. The Mayor welcomed us and we spent some time in his office. He even asked me to pray for his city. As we left, the Mayor asked if we would stop by at a local school where there was a ceremony in process celebrating the delivery

of some computers from friends in the US. We stopped by the celebration. In the fifteen minutes we were there, Dave Arnold met a lady from Washington DC and they exchanged business cards. That brief interchange resulted in a significant connection between the Nouveau Kiskeya project and the Haitian Ambassador to the United States.

As I wrestled with the massive disappointment of having to terminate our involvement in Nouveau Kiskeya, one question plagued me: *Where had God really been in all of this?* I shared some of my preliminary conclusions with our Board. These were my best attempts to explain the situation at the time:

"It appears that we are coming to the end of a major chapter in the life of the Nouveau Kiskeya project. Obviously the project didn't turn out the way we had hoped. I've thought a lot about that in the last year and the last 3 months and especially the last 30 days.

I'm still convinced that Nouveau Kiskeya was a God-inspired project but I do not understand why it ended up the way it ended up and maybe we never will. However, I think we can be encouraged by the fact that hundreds of people had jobs for a while, many people continue to have access to good water, two churches were birthed, at least 400 people were exposed to the message of Jesus, and 45 people converted from some form of voodooism to Christianity. This would include Innocent Duclos, the 72-year-old farmer who sold us the well property. Innocent died in November 2008 and is assumedly in heaven because we were there. One of our goals was to create jobs, but I suspect that in God's economy one soul trumps a thousand jobs, so there is no question in my mind that God's will was done."

I then reflected on how we should look back on this experience. I suggested that "it is easy to look back with bitterness; the government did not cooperate, we didn't always get the information we needed even from our partners, some of the information we got was not accurate. Lots of reasons to be bitter. However, bitterness does not accomplish anything, but grace glorifies God so I think we have to choose to look back with grace."

Once the legal details were finalized I found myself with a lot of time on my hands. Over the last three-and-a-half years Nouveau Kiskeya had consumed at least 80% of my working hours. Now my daily "to do" list, which had been extensive, was pretty much blank. The one thing that consumed my thinking was this one question: "Had Nouveau Kiskeya really been a God-project?"

In July 2009, though still exhausted, my wrestling resulted in the following honest admissions:

> "I allowed Haiti to consume my life."
>
> "I allowed Nouveau Kiskeya to become my sole source of purpose and meaning."
>
> "I probably, subconsciously, allowed this to happen because I was convinced that I was doing 'God Work.'"
>
> "God seemed to be blessing what we were doing which

> *I read as affirmation that we were doing the right thing ..."*

Then I added:

> *"If I were to assess my reaction to all of the above right now I would say that I am angry at the Haitian government leaders because they would not cooperate, and at God because He seemed to be sending mixed signals."*

From September 8, 2005 through April 30, 2009 I had embarked on a journey convinced that God had given it His unequivocal blessing. I had invested 43 months of my life and a substantial amount of my own money. I had also helped raise millions of dollars from other committed Christian investors, assuring them that "*if* we believe that this is a God-project, and I believe it is, there is no risk." Now all I had left was a question that kept spinning around in my head: "Had God really been in it?"

Attempting to find the answer would take me to a dark and empty place.

CHAPTER 8

Defend the cause of the weak and fatherless;
maintain the rights of the poor and oppressed.
Rescue the weak and needy;
deliver them from the hand of the wicked.

PSALM 82:3-4

Questioning God

I SCOURED MY HAITI JOURNEY FROM BEGINNING TO END attempting to answer the two questions that had begun to hound me: where was God in all this, and had I misinterpreted the signals along the way? I could find nothing to contradict my belief that God had called me to Haiti in 1999, directed my involvement with Partners Worldwide, and had directed the creation of Rescue One as well as my foray into Haitian politics and then the Nouveau Kiskeya land development project.

It was through our political involvement in 2005 that I met Robert and discovered that he and I shared the same vision I had expressed in my letter to Doug Seebeck in 2004. I then reviewed the "Miracle List." Sixteen in less than three years seemed to stretch the bounds of mere coincidence.

The fact that all this evidence supported my original premise only made my dilemma worse. If God had truly been behind this endeavor since its inception in 2005, and if He had repeatedly orchestrated circumstances to keep pushing us forward, how then could it have failed?

I had always operated from the premise that God's sovereign plans and purposes cannot be preempted by human or spiritual intervention. Nevertheless, I was left with three options: either Satan or Haitian officials were stronger than God; God was not in it, at all — something the facts would not allow me to accept; or maybe my faith in God had been entirely misplaced.

Over those bleak months this last option seemed to be the most compelling. I began to be plagued by mental attacks I could not deflect. They were ever present:

> *If God is a loving God do you really believe he would bring hope to thousands of poor people and then dash their dreams against the rocks?*
>
> *What concrete evidence do you have proving that the "miracles" were not just coincidences?*
>
> *How do you reconcile an omnipotent and sovereign God with apparent failure?*
>
> *How do you really know that what you've been told about God is true?*
>
> *Face it — is there really a God after all?*

My Christian friends tried to help by assuring me that "God's ways are not our ways." They responded to my deep discouragement with what felt like trite and superficial assurances: "God isn't finished with this project yet." "Trust God." "It will all make sense later." "God doesn't make any mistakes." But none of that well-meaning Christian rhetoric was able to put a dent in the despair and confusion caused by the total collapse of what I once believed had been a God sanctioned project.

I started to ask myself whether my entire faith had been founded on a mirage. This led me to entertain serious doubts about God. His non-existence seemed to be the most logical explanation for what had transpired. Perhaps there was no omnipotent Deity at work behind the scenes after all. Perhaps no God had inspired me (or anybody else) to dream about new political, economic or spiritual possibilities for this nation. Wasn't it more likely that it was either just an audacious idea or the self-aggrandizing vision of an American businessman with a Type-A personality?

I was raised in a Christian home and had thought of myself as a Christian all my life. The existence of God was the foundational premise to everything I believed. There have been times that I've questioned some of the stories in the Bible, but I never doubted the existence of God. For the first time in my life I wasn't so sure. Over those hopeless months, while I did not become an actual atheist, these unrelenting attacks pushed me to accept the logic of agnosticism and certainly that of a serious skeptic.

Since I'm an analytical guy I tend to quantify things. During my journey into this dark cavern I formulated and then monitored my faith/doubt index. At first, after we had decided to withdraw from the Nouveau Kiskeya project, my faith/doubt index hovered around 70/30 in favor of faith. But as the questions persisted without any satisfactory answers it had slid down to 30/70. There were many days when it plunged even lower. The scale I had designed reflected the condition of my heart. There was no way to avoid the reality: my faith was being overpowered by doubt. I felt like I had been thrown into a deep well, a cover had been slammed on top, and all light had been extinguished. It was a horrible experience.

Not only was my belief system turned upside down, the very core of my being had been shaken. It was as if the very foundation of who I was had been kicked out from under me. I felt empty and directionless. Like a compass without a magnetic field, I spun aimlessly. All familiar landmarks had been eradicated and I seemed to be wandering in a dense, unfamiliar, and frightening forest.

But, as irrational as it may seem, within me burned a longing to have my faith back. Not only that, I wanted something richer and deeper. I prayed not only that my faith would return but that it would be more vibrant than it had ever been. I prayed desperately to the God I wasn't sure I even believed in. I did not see this as faith. I did not recognize that this is perhaps the deepest type of faith: holding on to something or Someone that every shred of logic demands you reject. But nothing changed. At some point I asked myself a question: "Am I facing something more than mere depression and intellectual doubt? Is this something more evil and personal? Could I actually be experiencing a malicious spiritual battle?

From the little I knew I began to suspect that I might be in the middle of a full-out demonic attack. I started to take seriously the possibility that it was Satan who had been using distraction, discouragement, distrust, division, deception and depression in an attempt to destroy what we were trying to do in Haiti, and destroy me in the process.

I had blamed a greedy and arrogant cabinet minister for the project's death, but perhaps he was not the real enemy after all. Perhaps there had been evil, spiritual forces behind all the resistance we had experienced as well as this concentrated assault on my core beliefs. I couldn't be certain but down deep, when I became quiet enough, I somehow knew that this was the case.

Coming to this conclusion did not stop the attacks. If anything, they became even more intense. I was stressed and harassed constantly. It felt like there was someone latched onto my shoulder, 24/7, with a quiet, persistent, merciless voice, insinuating questions in my ear:

Why would a good God allow a project like Nouveau Kiskeya to fail?

Why doesn't God answer the prayers of the Haitian people?

Is it really true that there is a God who listens to and answers prayer?

During the worst of it I wrote in my journal, "God does not appear to be near, or anywhere. He does not appear to be answering my prayers. He does not appear to be providing any direction. It appears that He has taken things away but has not provided anything new in its place. Does God really exist?"

In an attempt to bolster what little faith remained, I began reading a series of books on Christian apologetics. All this reading led me to a simple conclusion: one cannot prove either the existence or the non-existence of God. However, as a result of this reading my faith/doubt index did begin to nudge upward just a bit.

Then, ironically, God used an avowed atheist to prod my faith higher by several more degrees. Matthew Parris, former British MP and London Times columnist, is a self-described atheist who grew up in Malawi, Africa. Though currently living in the UK he had returned to visit his birth country after a 45-year absence. In the summer of 2009 I "chanced" to come across an op-ed piece he had written for *The London Times.* Its timing was just as stunning as its title: "*As an atheist, I truly believe that what Africa needs is God.*"

This secular journalist's startling conclusion was clear and unapologetic. He wrote: "I've become convinced of the enormous contribution that Christian evangelism makes in Africa; sharply distinct from the work of secular NGOs, government projects and international aid efforts. These alone will not do. Education and training alone will not do. In Africa, Christianity changes people's hearts. It brings spiritual transformation. The rebirth is real. The change is good."

His scandalous thesis was based on an honest comparison of Christianity with the fatalistic mind-set inculcated by the traditional animistic religions. "Anxiety — fear of evil spirits, of ancestors, of nature and the wild, of tribal hierarchy, of quite everyday things — strikes deep into the whole structure of rural African thought." He observed that this world-view was the direct cause of a grinding and oppressive passivity that stunts any sense of personal initiative.

Sounding almost like an evangelist, Parris, the admitted atheist, describes the antidote: "Christianity, with its teaching of a direct, personal, two-way link between the individual and God, unmediated by the collective, and unsubordinated to any other human being, smashes straight through the philosophical/spiritual framework I've just described. It offers something to hold on to for those who are anxious to cast off a crushing tribal groupthink. That is why and how it liberates."

Parris admitted that he'd been trying to banish this belief his whole life. He conceded also that these conclusions embarrassed his "growing belief that there is no God." His statement haunted me and in a way bolstered my frail faith. I couldn't get it out of my mind. It wasn't long after that that I wrote the following in my journal:

"I truly believe that Haiti needs God."

and

"I truly believe that Ted needs God."

Though there was no drama, there was an overwhelming sense of peace. I simply decided to make a decision — I would choose to believe in God and accept the fact that He is a mystery that I cannot understand. Whether or not I would ever get any satisfactory answers to the questions that gnawed at me, whether I would be able to make any sense about what seemed to be the total collapse of our project, I would still place my faith in Him. It was a non-emotive leap of faith to trust in a God who was still hidden and silent.

While I would like to say that my faith/doubt index soared, that would not be true. What I can state is that over the next several months my faith continued inching upward by small degrees.

As hope was slowly rising in my heart, on January 12, 2010, a catastrophic 7.0 earthquake hit 16 miles west of Port-au-Prince killing somewhere between 100,000 to 300,000 people and leaving approximately 1,000,000 people homeless. When Robert informed us that many former Port-au-Prince families were fleeing to all parts of Haiti, including the Nouveau Kiskeya neighborhood, we decided to raise money through the Nouveau Kiskeya Foundation to provide jobs for as many people as we could to dig water retention canals and ponds. Priority hiring was offered to refugee families and to families hosting refugees.

Six months later, 17 water retention ponds had been dug, each approximately 435 feet long by 40 feet wide by 5 feet deep. Through strategically located canals, rainwater from the surrounding mountains would periodically fill these ponds. Their collective capacity was 6.6 million gallons. The water would be used to irrigate small gardens and provide water for countless farm animals. We also hired a Haitian agronomist to train 12 farmers in what for them were new methods of irrigation and crop-production. By the end of the project we had been able to employ 100 of the Port-au-Prince refugees for 100 days. They in turn had been able to take care of their families for over three months.

In retrospect I wonder whether being able to provide concrete assistance to desperate people was another means God used to strengthen my faith. By August of 2010, I was able to record in my journal that "I'm getting to the place where I am at peace with how the Nouveau Kiskeya project turned out. If God exists, I suspect that whatever He wanted to accomplish was accomplished or still will be. If He doesn't exist, I guess it doesn't matter. Just for the record, I believe that God exists."

I was also able to write; "my focus is more on the future than it is on the past and I have made a commitment to:

> Put my complete trust in God.
> Try not to figure things out by myself.
> Ask God what He wants me to do in all circumstances.
> Expect that God will tell me what to do."

> (PARAPHRASE OF PROVERBS 3:5)

I also began praying the following prayer to the God whose existence I still occasionally doubted:

> Yahweh, You are my God.
> Fill me with Your Holy Spirit.
> Surround me with the love of Jesus.
> Show me what it is that you want me to do.
> And gently direct my path.

> (PARAPHRASE OF PSALM 143:10)

As I was finding precarious hand-holds to drag myself out of the bleak cavern, I decided to share the *London Times* article with Robert. Since Haiti, despite being in the Western Hemisphere, is regarded by many as an African nation, I was curious to hear what he would make of Parris's conclusion. It was August 18, 2010.

I told him that in my devotional reading God had used Matthew 6:33 "Seek first His Kingdom" and Luke 12:31 "Seek the Kingdom of God above all else" to reinforce my growing sense that bringing God to the Nouveau Kiskeya neighborhood might be more important than providing water and vegetables or jobs.

I asked him what we could do to place the spiritual needs of the Haitian people on par with or perhaps even ahead of their physical needs. Borrowing the language of the writer from *The London Times* I wanted Robert's opinion about what we could do to "put even more focus on bringing God to the Nouveau Kiskeya neighborhood."

When I sent off the email I was not aware that Robert had been in conversation with a recent convert from voodoo that had left him shaken. In addition it had drastically shifted his perspective of his neighborhood and his nation. He responded less than eight hours later. What he wrote would have shocked me had we not shared a series of powerful and significant spiritual experiences over the years. Even so, his words sobered me.

What he told me contradicted all the prevailing wisdom about international relief work in Haiti. Actually, it ran contrary to most if not all the development theory I had been exposed to within the Christian community. And it raised the troubling issue of demons all over again.

If my people, who are called by my name,
will humble themselves and pray
and seek my face and turn from their wicked ways,
then will I hear from heaven and will forgive their sin
and I will heal their land.

2 CHRONICLES 7:13-14

CHAPTER 9

Three Questions about Poverty

IN ORDER TO EXPLAIN THE SIGNIFICANCE OF ROBERT'S response, I need to place it in its context. For almost ten years I had been working on a three-part puzzle about the roots of poverty. Even before deciding to invest myself in Haiti in 2002, I had struggled to come to terms with three fundamental questions:

"*Who are the poor of the 21st century?*"

"*Why are the poor, poor?*"

"*How do we help the poor?*"

Robert's reply was the next-to-last piece in solving this perplexing puzzle. Part of my motivation for traveling to Haiti had been to get some answers to these deceptively simple questions. Not surprisingly, when I landed in Port-au-Prince I saw and met many poor people, at least based on our North American standard. However, I was not convinced that being below the North American poverty line defined the poor of the 21st century. So, I dug a little deeper. I redefined my first question to: *Who are the poor of the 21st century **based on Biblical standards?***

The Bible doesn't define the poor as we tend to do today using the criterion of relative income levels. In the Bible, the poor are typically identified by their social and economic vulnerability. They are the weak, the alien, the fatherless and the widow — members of society who had nobody to protect them. When I reframed my question in the context of the vulnerable and the helpless while traveling the streets of Port-au-Prince in 2003, an answer leaped out at me: VULNERABLE CHILDREN are clearly poor based on the biblical standard. Even back in 2003 over 600,000 of Haiti's children were orphaned, disabled, abused or enslaved, and many lived in an orphanage, or on the street. (In the wake of the 2010 earthquake, that number has nearly doubled.) It required no stretch for me to conclude that many of Haiti's children easily fit the Biblical standard of "the poor".

Given this analysis I felt comfortable that I had found at least one answer to my initial question. I was confident that supporting and ministering to Haiti's disabled, abused, enslaved and orphan children honored the Biblical mandate to love mercy, rescue the weak and care for the poor. This realization became the major influence that led to the start-up of the Rescue One Children's Ministry in 2004. However, as an entrepreneur, I wanted to do more than address the needs of poor and vulnerable children; I wanted to eliminate the causes of poverty. This triggered the second question:

"Why are the poor, poor?"

I found that there are no easy answers to this question. There are countless books and articles on the subject and opinions range from one end of the spectrum to the other. Every expert has their own opinion, which frequently contradicts the opinions of the next expert. Very quickly I came to see that poverty is complex. Its causes cannot be reduced to a simple formula, and frequently not to one single cause. And it launched me on an extensive study that continues to this day.

I began to compile a list of the factors that contribute to poverty. I now refer to it as the Demons of Poverty and it includes the following:

- Corruption
- Injustice
- Inadequate Education
- Progress Resistant Religions
- Dysfunctional Government
- Class Based Society
- Colonialism (Historic and Current)
- Dependency
- Culture of Poverty

And this is only a partial list. What further complicates the issue is that these causes are inter-related and some "causes" are really symptoms of other causes. In addition, not all poverty is a result of all of these causes. Some poverty situations may have multiple causes and some might have single causes. However, two things occurred to me as I thought about this list; if you want to reduce poverty you need to address the causes of poverty, not just the symptoms and secondly, it occurred to me that there was a common denominator that linked all of these Demons of Poverty together. Behind each one of these Demons of Poverty stands the common cause of EVIL. That one common denominator provided a clue that would prove to be helpful as I began to think about my third question: *"How do we help the poor?"*

Unwittingly, even before getting on the plane for my first trip in 2003, I had started on a path toward discovering what I now consider to be a major influence behind systemic poverty in Haiti.

In preparation for my first visit I did some background reading. I wanted to have a better grasp of the history and culture of this mysterious country I was getting ready to visit. I read several books and, among other things, I learned that the major religious influence in that island nation was voodoo or "voudou", the French and Creole spelling — that comes from an African word for spirits. It is a syncretistic religion that has spliced together three different belief systems: African folklore which the slaves brought from Africa, West Indian legends, and elements of Roman Catholicism from their French slave owners. Most of what I read at that time convinced me that voodoo was a central but relatively harmless element of Haitian culture since its focus was on ancestor worship, appeasement of family spirits, and childish superstition. The main role of the priests or priestesses, I was told, is to protect people from spells. It was never made clear, nor did I think to ask, where did these spells, which required the intervention of counter-spells, originate? It also did not occur to me that choosing to become a voodoo priest or priestess was an income opportunity in a country with 80% unemployment.

According to the "experts," while there was a *bad* form of voodoo, what existed in Haiti was predominantly of the *good* variety. In my reading I did come across the curious fact that voodoo practitioners believed that spiritual power was centered at the crossroads where it is believed the natural and supernatural worlds converge.

In hindsight, I now realize I was seriously misled by what I read. Not only do I no longer believe that voodoo is culturally harmless, but almost ten years later I am convinced that there is no such thing as *good* voodoo. In fact I believe that it is one of the principal reasons for the unbroken shackles of poverty that have bound Haiti since it won its independence from France over two hundred years ago.

But, when I began my journey, I was convinced of the opposite. I accepted the opinions of the experts who assured me that voodoo was a quaint, traditional belief system — mostly superstition and minimally religious. I took them at their word; that is until August 18, 2010 when I received Robert's response to the Matthew Parris article.

He explained that he had been having a series of conversations with Luc, a local fisherman from Port-a-l'Ecu, who had recently been converted from voodoo to the Living God. Luc had been heavily involved in secret voodoo societies and had related some of the "wonders" he had been able to accomplish through the power given to him by voodoo spirits. He described meetings that he and others frequently attended by means of astral projection. Most disturbing were the rituals at the crossroads, which included murder and cannibalism.

Robert was astonished. Despite spending most of his life in Haiti, he admitted, "there is so much that I (at the age of 52) do not know about my own country and my own people. The most astonishing fact I learned about my people is how pervasive the presence of evil-practicing secret societies is within our culture. The country is littered with networks that are in contact with each other locality by locality." Robert was stunned to discover that around the Nouveau Kiskeya property there were at least ten of these secret societies.

As a result of these conversations and others that confirmed much of what he had been told, Robert told me that he had developed an action plan based on his study of Deuteronomy 18:9-14 and Deuteronomy 28:15-68. These passages describe the "detestable" occult practices of the Canaanites that had brought down God's curse and judgment on any Israelite who participated in them. The latter passage lists the horrible curses that would befall the nation of Israel were its people to forsake their God and follow other gods by engaging in these "detestable" practices.

"Haiti is under a curse," Robert declared, "and until the

pervasive 'detestable' voodoo practices of Deuteronomy 18:9-14 are stopped, Haiti will continue to be plagued with the curses of Deuteronomy 28:15-68 ... The resolution I have made before the Lord is to embark, in His Name, on a mission that will go from a public denunciation of the 'detestable' practices of voodoo in and around the Nouveau Kiskeya community to a one year campaign of public repudiation of those practices in our neighboring communities."

What astonished me was that even before Robert received my email in August of 2010 about increasing our commitment to bring God to the Nouveau Kiskeya neighborhood, he had already decided to engage in a campaign to dedicate the whole area to God.

His strategy was to enlist the help of the leaders of seven local churches and invite them to monthly meetings for worship, prayer and repentance for ten months. Then, on July 21st, 2011, for seven consecutive days, they would gather the membership of these sponsoring churches at seven major cross-roads in the district "to repudiate the 'detestable practices' in our midst just like Elijah did in 1 Kings 18."

The final piece of the puzzle that helped me formulate an answer to my third question (How do we help the poor?) fell into place in May of 2011. It provided an unexpected confirmation to my conclusion that, in the case of Haiti, there was one Demon of Poverty that stood out above the others.

A friend of mine referred me to a book whose title would have been enough for me to dismiss it. It was *The Central Liberal Truth,* written by Lawrence E. Harrison, the director of the Cultural Change Institute at the Fletcher School at Tufts University in Massachusetts. It turned out to be a watershed book for me and, despite its somewhat misleading title; it wasn't pushing a liberal agenda at all. Its aim was to understand why some countries are poor and others are not.

Harrison begins by analyzing the world's primary religions and discusses whether they are progress promoting or progress-resistant. His conclusion is as startling as it was refreshing: "The single biggest determinant of a country's wealth versus poverty is culture and one of the biggest influences on culture is religion." In all my study I had never heard that before.

Most interesting for me was his use of Haiti as an illustrative model. He had lived and worked there and analyzed the country through the eyes of an anthropologist. He also raised essentially the same question I had been asking:

> "Why does this island nation remain the least developed country in the Western Hemisphere despite having received billions of dollars in foreign aid over the last 50 years? Why has Haiti consistently defied all development prescriptions?"

After carefully evaluating the role of voodoo and other animist religions he concludes that, compared to all other religions, they exert the worst influence on progress. His thesis was startling: "Animist religions (voodoo), in which what happens in life is determined by a pantheon of capricious spirits, present an extreme case of progress-resistant culture, as we have seen in Haitian Voodoo." (Culture Matters, Kindle Location 2585) He quotes Cameroonian development expert Daniel Etounga-Manguelle who states that, "A society in which magic and witchcraft flourish is a sick society ruled by tension, fear, and moral disorder." (Kindle Location 2585).

Harrison's conclusion affirmed what Matthew Parris had observed and what Robert had recently discovered. In an article published later, entitled "Haiti and the Voodoo Curse," Harrison observed that "Because Haiti's culture is powerfully influenced by its religion, voodoo … it is without ethical content. Its followers believe that their destinies are controlled by hundreds of capricious spirits who must be propitiated through voodoo ceremonies." He identifies voodoo as a type of sorcery religion and indicates "that is one of the principal obstacles to progress in Africa," and by implication the nation of Haiti. "Haiti-and-the-Voodoo-Curse" (http://fletcher.tufts .edu).

Thus, I was given the answer to my most perplexing question by an internationally respected sociologist, who as far as I know has no theistic bias. According to him, the poor in Haiti are poor because of their set of values, beliefs and attitudes, rooted in a religion that profoundly impacts the way its adherents think and act, creating a mind-set that stubbornly resists progress.

Behind this pervasive poverty was a way of thinking about life, and behind that world-view was a religion. Harrison's study affirmed what Robert and I had come to suspect. One of the most significant influences behind Haitian poverty was a nation-wide commitment to a religion of fear, futility and fatalism.

To me it was ironic that two authors, neither one of which

had a religious agenda, had come up with an astonishing theistic answer to my third question; "How do we help the poor?" "What Africa needs", (in Parris's words) "is God" and "What countries like Haiti need", (in Harrison's words) "is to encourage conversion of those practicing animist religions to more progress-prone religions [like Christianity]." (Kindle Location 2585)

This revelation was shocking but it should not have been since I started this journey motivated by my Christian faith. But knowing what I know now, I am ready to accept that the formula for our entry into Haiti ten years earlier might have been backwards. We had gone in to bring a lot of jobs and a little bit of God. Maybe what Haiti really needed was a more intentional focus on God and perhaps a secondary focus on jobs. If Parris and Harrison and Robert were right in their diagnosis of the problem, then the country was in need of more focus on doing exactly what Robert started doing deliberately in 2010 ... breaking down the historic strongholds and replacing them (in the words of Lawrence Harrison) with a "more progress-prone religion, like Christianity".

So is Christianity the solution to world poverty? I don't know about the world but when it comes to Haiti; that is where I am putting my time and money. In addition to rescuing vulnerable children we are involved in a major initiative to strengthen Christian churches in Northwest Haiti that I truly believe will have long term impact and eternal results. Will it reduce Haitian poverty? Yes, I believe it will. If we can help people understand that God endowed them with the ability and the responsibility to take care of themselves, their families and their environment, and if people begin to believe that they can make a difference in their own lives and that they have a responsibility to help their family and their neighbors, I believe that the power of historic strongholds can be broken and the Haitian people also can be on their way to social and economic progress.

The one who calls you is faithful,
and he will do it.
1 THESSALONIANS 5:24

CHAPTER 10

Reflections

IN 2002 I HAD BEGUN WITH GREAT HOPES, HIGH EXPECTA-
tions and tremendous optimism expecting that, as a Christian businessman, I could do something to make a positive contribution in an impoverished island nation off the Florida coast. Having been successful as an entrepreneur in the U.S., I had been confident that I could transfer what I had learned to help others succeed in their country.

My assumption was that general principles of business growth can be applied broadly and implemented carefully in a variety of nations, geographies and cultures. I had not stopped to articulate it but had I done so it would have been something like: Business principles are universal — what has helped grow my business *here* can be used by another dedicated entrepreneur to succeed *there*.

It sounds logical and looks good on paper. It has a common sense appeal, after all, as we frequently hear: Business is Business. However, the reality is much different. It took me ten years to discover this and, for a time, it almost cost me my faith.

As I reflect on my experiences and my desire to use my entrepreneurial skills to help create jobs for the poor, I now realize that I lacked vital information. I did not know what I did not know and much of what I thought I knew was incorrect. From a purely investment perspective I was violating a cardinal rule: investing without fully understanding the investment: its purpose, its cost, its challenges, its extent, and its components. I was essentially gambling on an unknown enterprise, rather than investing wisely with both eyes open.

There are a number of crucial truths I wish I had known before jumping into this international job-creation project. (I share these in more detail in the "Practical Lessons Learned" section of this book.) These are truths I learned the hard way. They are principles that any well-intentioned Christian, desiring to use business as mission (to use a phrase that is becoming increasingly popular), would benefit from knowing at the front-end. They certainly would have kept me from a great deal of frustration, confusion and disappointment. They might not have guaranteed success for the Nouveau Kiskeya project, but they could have saved me from entering a tunnel that almost swallowed me whole. My hope is that they may provide a similar service to you.

One of the most important lessons that came out of my ten-year odyssey in Haiti was the recognition of how easy it is for our pride to sneak its way even into a God-inspired mission. Perhaps that is the one essential lesson that God was after all along. As I read over my journal of those years I now see how most of my struggles resulted from my unwillingness to "let go and let God." My Dutch, Calvinistic, ingrained sense of responsibility made the concept of surrender elusive and, at points, incomprehensible.

At the end of 2008, after almost a full year of unceasing conflict and confusion, I confessed in my journal what had been true for me since I had made a serious commitment to work in Haiti seven years earlier:

> "I pray as if everything is dependent on God but I act as if everything is dependent on me. I need to get my praying and my acting in sync. Even one of my favorite Scripture passages (Psalm 143:10) suggests that we should only do what God shows us that we should do and where we feel the guiding of the Holy Spirit directing our path. We pray 'show us what it is You want us to do' and then still proceed to do it our way."

We, who live in a rich and comfortable nation, especially people like myself who are used to seeing problems as challenges that can and will be overcome, and who look at the future with optimism rather than fear, are frequently unaware of the depth of our unhealthy sense of self-confidence.

Even if we verbally affirm our dependence on God and our recognition of His blessing, underneath runs a powerful current that is energized much more by ego and pride than by God's Spirit. While we may say our confidence and our trust is in Him, at the core of our being what we are actually depending on are our own gifts, abilities, skills, techniques, and frequently, money. Maybe it is this unconscious idolatry that God wanted to expose.

In the summer of 2009 I was asked to give a talk in Toronto about the Bible passage in Matthew 19:24 that says "it is easier for a camel to go through the eye of a needle than for a rich man to enter the kingdom of God." My focus was on what Saint Matthew may have been referring to when he used the term "rich man." After giving it much thought I concluded that what he really meant by the "rich" was the "self-sufficient." By definition, the self-sufficient don't need God. As I prepared that talk I realized that I was talking to myself.

For 42 months I had struggled to launch the Nouveau Kiskeya project and although I had frequently acknowledged that it was a "God-project" I never got to the point where I could simply let go. Looking back, I now realize that what was exposed in that painful process was how my own identity was wrapped up in *doing* rather than in simply *being* available to be used by God to accomplish His purposes.

One of my last journal entries in 2009, the year that we closed the doors on Nouveau Kiskeya and the year my faith was almost extinguished, was a quote from Henri Nouwen, one of my favorite authors. It addresses this internal conflict that believers of all ages have had to face. It lies at the core of the difference between those who become saints and those who do not: "What fascinates me," Nouwen writes, "is that those whose whole mind and heart were directed to God had the greatest impact on other people, while those who tried very hard to be influential (and successful) were quickly forgotten."

I will build my church;
*and the **gates of hell** shall not*
prevail against it.
MATTHEW 16:18B

Epilogue

FROM SUNDAY JULY 24TH THROUGH SATURDAY JULY 30TH, 2011, somewhere between 1,000 and 2,000 Haitian Christians met daily to pray at one of the seven crossroads in the Nouveau Kiskeya neighborhood. They had been preparing for nine months for this "Spiritual Warfare Campaign" by gathering together regularly to worship, pray and fast. They were members of 40 local churches. In Haiti, the unity of their pastors and their commitment to one common cause was nothing short of a miracle in itself.

Robert Ulysse had spearheaded the campaign that quickly gained traction when he wrote and distributed what became known as the "Break Curses Prayer" taken from Deuteronomy 18 and 28. (A copy is included in the Appendix). It was a call to Haitian Christians to disavow their allegiance to the demonic spirits behind the national voodoo cult and to commit themselves unreservedly to the true and living God.

In effect, it was a repudiation and denunciation of what their forefathers had done over 200 years earlier when they renounced the "white man's God" and devoted themselves to their ancestral African spirits. It was a bold confrontation with the powers of darkness and a direct challenge to demonic powers that have kept that nation paralyzed by fear and locked in the unbreakable grip of crushing, systemic poverty.

Midway through the campaign the power of God was already being manifest. Robert reported that, "Several voodoo practitioners have confided to me that voodoo worshipers are experiencing great difficulty in getting their gods to respond when they are called upon during their recent nightly voodoo services." With growing confidence, born of seeing God's power revealed, he continued, "Since voodoo services cannot begin until the voodoo god in whose honor the service is being held comes down and possesses a worshiper and then speaks through that worshipper, this is getting the attention of the voodoo community."

The seven-day campaign concluded on a triumphant note of victory. A voodoo priest named Solivert Joseph came forward with his wife to declare that they wanted to renounce their voodoo practices in favor of the "Living God." Exuberant believers packed three pickup trucks to drive to their home where all their occult articles were removed and burned.

Robert explains the significance of what occurred in light

of the dark forces that have kept his nation in bondage for centuries:

> "Voodoo keeps people in bondage through fear. Haitians in general fear the power of voodoo more than they fear God. Crossroads are known to be the seats of power of the meanest spirits of voodoo. Many people believe that anyone who would dare attack the voodoo spirits on their turf (the crossroads) would be severely punished.

> Some people clearly said that they would wait to see if we could really hold the services at the crossroads without anyone among us being struck dead right there. Therefore, one of our prayers has been that the 'Living God' would keep us free from any type of harm, even the simplest incident or accident, since any incident would be interpreted as a punishment. By the grace of God, we ended the seven days without even a minor incident even though over-loaded pickup trucks and busses carried thousands of people over mountainous and other potentially treacherous roads. So our God answered our prayers."

What took place at these crossroads (and what did not) spread like a flash flood throughout the entire region. Its impact was profound and shook entrenched beliefs. The dark forces controlling the lives of men, women, crops and animals had been directly and publicly confronted.

As a result of their direct defiance of the voodoo spirits, Robert reported that "the general belief in our region after the crossroad events is that Satan should not be feared if one believes in the 'Living God.'" Since that time many have continued to turn from the power of darkness to serve the Living God.

At the outset of our plan to create an economic hub that would transform a slice of oceanfront regarded by its neighbors as cursed, I had an audacious idea: I wanted to dramatically illustrate God's sovereignty over the Nouveau Kiskeya property. I decided that we would erect a cross that would overshadow the whole development. To accomplish this task I requested that a group of Calvin College engineering students put their minds to work on how to make it happen.

It took them a semester of investigation but they finally figured it out. It would require a cross 82 feet tall, and wide enough for an interior staircase to the top. Windows on the horizontal and vertical axes would shine rectangles of light, visible along the entire length of Nouveau Kiskeya. Ocean liners and cruise boats, five miles off the coast, would see it too. Over and above what was projected to be thousands of homes — hundreds of luxury dwellings and businesses, along with ports of call crowded with tourists, residents and workers — would stand the cross of Christ. It would shine brightly where once only death, darkness and a paralyzing fear reigned.

In my office stands the model of the cross the students built for the project. It measures about 32 inches tall. I wonder whether the campaign to push back the darkness around Nouveau Kiskeya has at last laid the real groundwork for the fulfillment of that original vision. Was it worship and prayer that God was really after? And will it be those spiritual weapons that needed to be unsheathed before the demonic power behind the poverty that holds millions of Haitians captive could be exposed, denounced and laid low?

It is possible that there will come a day in which this thin forgotten strip of land which was once used as a curse word will have the shadow of a cross resting on it — literally. And it will be a sign and a wonder. It will be a mighty symbol of resurrection. But if not, I know that already the cross of Christ has been raised up in the hearts of thousands. It is already declaring the message that out of defeat, victory comes; that out of failure, and despair, and hopelessness, life and joy and hope burst forth from the darkest grave.

Through the commitment of thousands of believers who have devoted themselves to reclaim their land from Satan, his vice-like grip is being broken. Their praises have lifted the cross high to proclaim the good news that upon a people living in the deepest, demonic darkness a great light has shined. And it has put on public display, for all who have eyes to see, that the Message of Jesus is truly good news for the poor. For this message does more than create jobs; it brings freedom from fear and a promise of an abundant life, both here and forever. It is an emancipation proclamation for those with little as well as those with much. It is a guarantee that sin, Satan, and all his hosts, have been defeated and that even now, despite all appearances, the Lord of Life, who is Lord of all, reigns. This is good news indeed — for the poor *as well as for the rich.*

Another Side of the Story

by Jan Boers

"DEMONS OF POVERTY" IS OBVIOUSLY WRITTEN FROM TED'S point of view. It is the story that only he can tell. Running parallel to his story and his perceptions there is another story. It is the story that only I can tell.

Ten years ago when Ted became involved in various projects in Haiti, our knowledge of the country was rudimentary. We knew that Haiti was a very poor nation with a history of corruption. We knew that there was something called "voodoo" that permeated the lives of the Haitian people. That was about all we knew.

Ten years later, we know quite a bit more. We have had glimpses into the lives of the Haitian people, their culture, their politics and their religious beliefs. I also have come to the conclusion that the people of Haiti are living in a spiritual war zone.

"Spiritual Warfare" is a term that I had heard thrown around in Christian circles most of my life. The idea that there are good spirits and evil spirits fighting to control the lives of us earthlings seemed a little Star-Warsish to me, so for many years I simply ignored it. Later I began to realize that when one makes an attempt to claim for God something that Satan has claimed for his own, one has entered a war zone.

After Ted and I were married and had three children, I became an inspirational speaker and Bible Study lecturer. I had been warned by speakers whom I respected that I could expect both testing and an encounter with spiritual warfare when I entered this area of ministry. I can't say that I was overly concerned about this, but I soon learned that their warnings were warranted.

I shudder when I recall the series that I led on the Fruit of the Spirit. During a nine-week series, I planned to present lectures on how each aspect of the Fruit of the Spirit could be demonstrated in the lives of Christian women. However, during those nine weeks, my "Love, Joy, Peace, Patience, Kindness, Goodness, Faithfulness, Gentleness, and Self-Control" were all put to the test. Each and every week, I struggled with the attribute of the Fruit that I was supposed to be demonstrating. People I found difficult to love seemed to appear from nowhere on the week that I was to speak about Love. Where was my Joy and Peace during the weeks that I was supposed to be teaching others about demonstrating these attributes? And so it went for nine long weeks.

Although it was difficult, I realized that these tests were necessary for me both individually and as a teacher. I had never planned to present myself as a woman who had it all together. Anyone who knows me knows that that isn't true! I needed to experience failure in each area as a reminder that it is only through God's Spirit within us that we can overcome the trials found in our daily lives.

It was during this time of testing that I first felt myself vulnerable to Satan's attack. He seemed to be constantly whispering in my ear insinuating that my failures disqualified me from teaching or leading. I needed to be reminded that God's Spirit gently rebukes when we err, but the Enemy sends feelings of guilt and defeat. The affirmation I received from God's Word and the encouragement I received from others allowed me to recognize this as Satan's attempt to keep me from doing what my God had planned for me to do. It was a valuable lesson that I would need to draw upon as we began to work in Haiti. My encounter with spiritual warfare had begun.

These minor skirmishes did not adequately prepare me for the attack that would take place when Ted became committed to working in Haiti. I had never experienced an attack that was so personal and so debilitating. As a woman, I am protective of my role in our marriage. I soon felt that my role was being minimized. My daily activities revolved around activities that could be deemed necessary but mundane. I felt like Ted was focused on saving the world while the only thing I was saving was a few dollars at the grocery store. Since I believed that God had called me to be a wife, mother, grandmother, daughter and homemaker, I should have recognized these feelings as a tactic of the Enemy.

As a wife, I tend to be protective of my husband. When I saw Ted being consumed by his commitments to Haiti to the detriment of his health and our relationship, I became resentful. Satan was right there to latch on to that resentment. He had a field day as Ted and I struggled to determine and then submit to God's will for our lives. It wasn't an easy thing to do. It still isn't. However, we are more successful in recognizing the Enemy's attempts to prevent our submission to God's will today than we were back then.

Background

If there are two ways of doing things, you can be sure that Ted and I will each choose the opposite way. Early in our marriage, we were two independent individuals who frequently questioned our compatibility. As we matured, we began to appreciate God's perfect plan for us. We discovered that we were meant to complement rather than to compete with each other. While Ted prefers to focus on the big picture, my natural inclination is to focus on the details. Coming to this realization gave us a greater appreciation for each other and the unique partnership that God had brought together.

When Ted began toying with the idea of involvement in Haiti, I was not overly thrilled with the idea. Until this point in our marriage, Ted had been focused on building a business to provide for our family and he had been involved in various ministries. Never one to do things half-heartedly, his involvement was always all-consuming. My focus on our family and a drama/speaking ministry was equally absorbing.

The Half-Time Seminar we attended in 2001 made us both desire to find something significant that we could do together. The problem would be finding that "something."

While Ted's hands-on responsibility to our business was

diminishing, my family obligations were increasing. By 2002, when the door to Haiti seemed to be opening for Ted, our family had grown from three adult children to include two children-in-law and four grandchildren. During the next eight years of our involvement that number would increase to include another son-in-law and four more grandchildren. My aging mother was also showing signs of Alzheimer's and I had taken on extra responsibilities for her.

In addition to that, I was diagnosed with an early stage of breast cancer that required a mastectomy and a radical surgical reconstruction. Ted was protective of me those first few difficult weeks and months of recovery. Surprisingly, his desire to protect me later became another tool that Satan would use against us in our spiritual battle.

My fear was that our desire to work on something significant together would be eclipsed by Ted's urgency to begin the second half of his life and my reluctance to take that next step. I was involved in, feeling called to, and loving my own comfortable world. Yet, I also wanted more than anything else to be part of this new venture he was undertaking.

The Battle Begins

In marriage, God takes two uniquely gifted *individuals* and allows them to become a uniquely gifted *team*. That team is able to do far more than they could accomplish as separate individuals. This is what Solomon refers to in Ecclesiastes 4:9-12 when he describes the cord of many strands that is not easily broken.

During our forty-four years of marriage, Ted and I have learned some valuable lessons. One is to appreciate the gifts that each of us brings into our partnership. We agree that some of the things that I can offer are:

> A different point of view
>
> Another set of eyes
>
> Another pair of ears
>
> A feminine perspective and
>
> That mysterious gift we call "Women's intuition."

That is why I was so taken aback when Ted decided to take his first trip to Haiti without me. Because he had heard of the difficult and demanding conditions that might be encountered, he was concerned that my recent surgeries had left me too weakened for the rigors of the trip. I didn't agree, but I didn't insist upon coming along. I should have. Instead I allowed a seed of resentment to be planted in my heart. Satan made sure that seed would have ample opportunity to flourish.

Upon his return home, Ted found a wife who was less than enthusiastic about his adventure. One positive outcome of the hurt caused by this first trip was our agreement that since we were a team, he would encourage me to travel with him on all subsequent trips. As a result of this experience, we learned two valuable lessons. The first lesson was that one of Satan's tactics is to divide and conquer. The second lesson was that we function best as a team. Together we are better able to assess situations than either of us could alone.

The Campaign Year

As Ted describes, 2005 was our political year in Haiti. During that time, we were invited to attend an outdoor political rally where a Christian leader would be announcing his candidacy for President. The meeting was supposed to begin mid-afternoon to allow the attendees sufficient time to return home before it became dark. These were days when there was a great deal of political unrest in Haiti so traveling after sunset was considered unwise.

I would guess that there were several thousand people in attendance at this rally. At least, it looked like thousands to me as I viewed the crowd from the platform that held the "dignitaries" who were attending. Ted and I, and an internationally known pastor were the only white people on that platform. A wall of what I later described as "very black men in very black uniforms with very black military guns" separated us from the crowd. I couldn't help but wonder, "What are we doing here?" It wasn't fear that prompted that question. I can only describe the feeling I was experiencing as surreal.

Since Haitian culture is not known for punctuality, it should have been no surprise to us that darkness was upon us before it was time to leave for the safety of our hotel. Although Ted was oblivious to it, I sensed that our Haitian friend was extremely uncomfortable as he inched his vehicle through the people who were thronging the street. It was then that I sensed something for the first time. I could only describe it as a palpable presence of evil. Shadowy forms passing by our windows seemed to have an ominous, oppressive power. I mentioned my feelings to Ted later in the evening, but he was too caught up in the political excitement to take much stock in my foreboding.

For many, this was the day that a Christian candidate announced his desire to be President of Haiti. For me, it was the day that the Enemy announced that he was already very present in Haiti. It was unsettling.

Learning through Immersion

It was on a wintry night in March of 2004 that Ted and I sat at the airport in Grand Rapids, awaiting the arrival of the storm-delayed airplane carrying our Haitian guest. She would be living with us for the next three months. The reality of the commitment we had made to take this young woman under our protection began to hit us.

We had only had two or three brief encounters with Kerline before inviting her to stay with us. On a recent visit to Port-au-Prince, we had had dinner with Kerline and her husband Lesly. He had casually mentioned her need to learn English in order to enhance her career opportunities. Kerline's English skills at that point were elementary, but she seemed determined to improve her employment prospects by becoming fluent in English.

On our flight home the next day, Ted and I were both preoccupied with our own thoughts. After a while, we looked at each other anticipating the conversation that would follow. Our lives were full, but we had an empty bedroom. We both felt that God was calling us out of our comfort zone. Although we thrive on privacy and alone time, we knew that we were supposed to offer our empty nest to this young woman. Shortly after our return home, an invitation was extended for Kerline to stay with us for three months of English immersion.

Originally, the plan had been for Kerline to stay with us during the summer months when our Michigan weather would be more comfortable for her. However, because unrest in Haiti was making it dangerous in the streets of Port-au-Prince, Lesly called and asked if Kerline could come immediately. As soon as a visa was acquired, Kerline was on her way.

It seemed to take forever for the passengers to disembark from the plane. It occurred to us that we might not even recognize our guest since our meetings had been so brief. Finally, a beautiful young Haitian woman made her way through the gateway. I think that we all wondered who would learn more during her months of English immersion ... her or us.

During the day, we learned about each other by observing habits and activities. It was in the evening during dinner that we learned about each other's cultures. It was only natural that the plight of Haiti's poor and orphaned children would be a recurring topic of conversation.

As we talked about Haitian children, I could vividly picture those we had seen on our visit to an orphanage on an earlier visit to Port-au-Prince. During these conversations we learned about the terrible abuses of the restavec system and the desperate needs of children in overcrowded orphanages. Ted and I both felt strongly moved to do something. That is what prompted us to launch Rescue One. Our goal was to provide food, healthcare, and a Christian education to the poorest of the poor children through local Haitian churches. Another major priority for us was to make it possible for these children to continue to live with their own families if that was feasible.

During our dinnertime conversations Kerline explained to us that while Haitian culture places a high value on family helping family, there was no corresponding sense of obligation to help anyone outside that bond. This was one of the new paradigms that Rescue One would introduce. In fact, it wasn't until Haitian churches embraced this model that individual church members began to understand their responsibility to those who were poorer than they — even ones to whom they were not related by blood.

After she returned to Haiti and the Rescue One program had been implemented, Kerline shared with us the moving experience of a Haitian doctor who served on a Rescue One church committee. The doctor admitted that she had never really given much thought to the poor in the church or its neighboring community until her involvement with Rescue One. She decided that she would offer free medical exams to the Rescue One children in their church program.

One morning when the doctor arrived at her office, there was an elderly woman awaiting her. The woman was the grandmother of a Rescue One student whom the doctor had examined some time before. In the grandmother's hand, there was a basket containing coffee, eggs and bread. Breakfast for the doctor. The grandmother explained that this gift was her way of showing appreciation for the services that had been rendered to her grandchild.

As the doctor humbly accepted the basket, pictures of the shack that the grandmother and child shared flashed through her mind. It was in a ravine that flooded with the city's foul sewage every time it rained. The fabric that covered the entrance to the shack offered no protection from inclement weather or intruders. The grandmother had so little and yet, out of gratitude, she shared a breakfast that was far beyond her means. The doctor told Kerline that her attitude to the poor would never be the same.

The Seductress

I'll admit it. I was becoming angry. In 1968, Ted and I had stood before our parents, our friends and our God repeating the vows that we had memorized. Those vows ended with "I hereby pledge to you my troth." I didn't know what troth meant then, but I was pretty sure that it had something to do with faithfulness to each other.

As I mentioned earlier, I am protective of my role as wife. As Ted's involvement in Haiti grew, I found that I was being consistently relegated to second place whenever there was a crisis. In my estimation, that meant about 100% of the time both day and night. Even when Ted was physically in my presence, it was obvious that his thoughts were elsewhere. He was no longer able to take joy in our family outings and get-togethers. It seemed he was becoming more and more withdrawn and preoccupied with Haiti.

I was conflicted because while this rejection hurt deeply, I felt it was selfish to resent Ted's ever-increasing involvement in something he felt God had called him to do. I resented that my husband, on a daily basis, was putting that country's needs before mine. I began to look upon Haiti as a seductress who controlled my husband's every moment. When I saw the toll his imbalanced commitment was having on his physical and emotional health, I grew even more angry.

Of course, Satan took full advantage of these feelings and the breach they were creating between us. My resentment reached a head one afternoon as Ted was making arrangements for yet another trip to Haiti. As I recall, it would take place over a 4th of July weekend celebration.

When Ted looked up from his desk, he saw the turmoil and frustration that I was experiencing. In that moment he realized that his life was out of balance. That realization was followed by a sense of hopelessness for there didn't seem to be any way of regaining control. He reacted by saying, "This isn't worth the pain that you are going through."

As he said this, a quote from Oswald Chambers flashed through my mind. "If we obey God, it is going to cost other people more than it costs us and that is where the pain begins." January 11, "My Utmost for His Highest"

If Ted and his friends were making a difference in the lives of the Haitian people, I could not allow Satan a victory by forcing Ted to withdraw from his commitment and calling. Even though I didn't want him to go, I told him that he had to book the flight.

It was a painful time. I sought Christian counseling that

resulted in Ted and I setting up boundaries that included Haiti-free time. It wasn't easy, but we were again united in our desire to continue our Haitian journey together.

The Meeting

We refer to the momentous audience with Prime Minister Madame Pierre-Louis and her cabinet on January 29, 2009 as "The Meeting." While Ted and the team were at the Prime Minister's office I stayed behind at the Montana Hotel. Although I had no way of knowing the details of what was taking place, I had a certainty about what its outcome would be. There were two things of which I was absolutely convinced: we were engaged in fierce spiritual warfare on Satan's turf and he would emerge the winner of this particular battle.

For quite some time, I had tried to convince Ted that the persistent barriers to the Nouveau Kiskeya project and the resistance we had been encountering were actually evidence of spiritual warfare. What I experienced at the hotel the morning of "The Meeting" was a direct confirmation of everything I had been telling him. For a fleeting moment, I thought I saw evidence of the Enemy himself.

Before I continue, I should explain that I have never had a supernatural vision. Prior to this experience, God allowed me to see Him through His Word and in everyday things. I feel closest to God when I am writing about seeing God in the ordinary and the mundane. For months prior to this trip, I had severe writer's block. During the days leading up to "the meeting," I had planned to lounge on a terrace overlooking

Port-au-Prince to relax and read. On one such day, I suddenly knew that the block was gone. I put down the book I had intended to read and began to write down one devotional after another on a yellow legal pad. As I wrote, I felt that God was allowing me to see Haiti through His eyes.

While Ted and the team were at "The Meeting," I decided to transcribe the devotions I had written from the legal pads onto the computer. While doing so, something unusual happened. I thought that I had actually seen something. This is how I would describe it the next day:

The Serpent

I had seen evidence of it before. Over the past seven years of our involvement in Haiti it was becoming more and more obvious that Haiti was a stronghold of demonic forces.

It was evident when we looked into the sub-human living conditions of Haiti's poor.

It was evident when we learned of the abuses and ritualistic mutilations of helpless children.

It was evident when we longed to help create jobs for the poor only to have the government tell us to cease and desist.

It was evident when we listened to the lies coming from the mouths of smiling government officials.

But it had never been so evident to me as on that day.

Even now, I find myself questioning my memory. It was only yesterday, but did I really see what I thought I saw?

I was passing time while Ted and the team made their presentation to the Prime Minister and members of her cabinet. I sat before the computer typing in handwritten devotional notes. Something appeared before my eyes within a two to three second flash. The only sound that I heard was a "swoosh" and it was gone.

This is what I saw … I saw a red-scaled serpent slither from the right side of the Prime Minister's Cabinet room. It coiled itself around the table where the Haitian government officials sat. From behind the officials, it raised its body until its head was level to theirs. Then its eyes looked piercingly at our team and its forked tongue shot out menacingly.

Did I really see that?
What was it I saw?
Could it simply have been a figment of my imagination?

I do not believe that what I saw that morning was a figment of my imagination. For a brief moment in time, I believe that God allowed me to see how the Enemy had infiltrated the government of Haiti.

After they read this description of what I saw, some friends asked if I was afraid for our team. I didn't experience any fear but rather a peace in knowing that our team was under God's protection.

When I saw the team upon their return from the Prime Minister's office, the term that came to mind was battle weary. They were in a state of disbelief and shock. Later, I was able to share with Ted what I had seen. He would no longer ignore the spiritual aspect of the battle he and the team had encountered.

Conclusion

I felt compelled to share this story because each of you, if you attempt to bring light and hope to people who are living in darkness and despair, will likely become targets of Satan's attack. Ephesians 6 describes the armor that God has given us for our protection and it is imperative that we are prepared to use it. Our faith in God and His promises is a shield that the Enemy cannot penetrate.

I am thankful that we, as Christians, can have the assurance that the battle ultimately belongs to the Lord. In the meantime I'm also thankful that because of God's plan, Ted and I are now on this battlefield together.

Where Do We Go from Here?

SO THAT IS OUR STORY. THANK YOU FOR READING IT. Although the telling of our story is finished for now, the story isn't over. In fact, the following events are just a few of the things that have happened recently:

On January 30, 2012 two representatives from the Timothy Leadership Training team in Port-au-Prince came to Nouveau Kiskeya. The purpose of their trip was to conduct a full week of Timothy Leadership training for the 40 church leaders that had been actively involved in the Spiritual Warfare campaign started by Robert Ulysse. The focus of this training, the first of six weeklong sessions over a period of three years, was on the critical function of Christian Pastors as role models, shepherds and servants to the people.

On July 2, 2012 Nouveau Kiskeya hosted the second week of Timothy Leadership Training events. The attendees reported that they could already see positive changes in their parishes with many more people committing their lives to the Living God, joining the church and becoming active in church and community affairs. The focus of the July training was to lay the Bible based groundwork for helping the church leaders realize that God would provide all their needs.

On March 14, 2012 Michel Joseph Martelly, the President of Haiti and some of his Cabinet members visited Nouveau Kiskeya by helicopter. The purpose of the President's visit was to promote his vision for a decentralized Haiti.

On June 16, 2012 we began a series of serious discussions about restarting the Nouveau Kiskeya project with an international development firm that has significant experience in Haiti.

If you are interested in the current status of the Nouveau Kiskeya project please check www.demonsofpoverty.com

The rest of this book is about what I learned on this journey. Some are lessons that deal with my faith journey and some are practical insights gleaned (by trial and error, success and failure) during our ten-year Haitian odyssey. I encourage you to read the rest of the book and I invite you to become part of this learning process. Whether you agree or disagree I would appreciate your input. There are no wasted experiences when we share what we learn with each other. To take part in this international dialogue, please go to www.demons ofpoverty.com

SPIRITUAL REFLECTIONS

There are several spiritual questions that I wrestled with as I processed the events of the last ten years. These were the dominant ones:

Does God really call people to specific tasks?

Can a God project fail?

Is it OK to doubt God?

The following is my attempt to answer these questions.

Does God Really Call People to Specific Tasks?

WHEN I EXAMINE THAT QUESTION IN LIGHT OF "MY CALL TO Haiti", I certainly have to admit that I did not hear an audible voice or have a vision of some angelic being giving me an assignment. But I did have a sense … a strong sense. Did God implant that sense? I don't really know but I think so. There is no other way that I can explain a sincere and unshake-able interest in a country I knew nothing about, that continues to this day. Also, there is no other way that I can explain the miraculous things that happened along the way or these indisputable results that are clear to me as I look back:

- at least 75 kids were rescued from a life of abject poverty.

- Innocent Duclos and possibly others are in Heaven because we were there.

- 100 plus voodoo practitioners and several voodoo priests converted to Christianity.

- 37 boat people who were trying to get from Haiti to the Bahamas washed up on the Nouveau Kiskeya beach and were rescued from possible death after 5 days at sea.

- hundreds of people in our neighborhood were provided employment for several years as we cleared land, built roads and developed a guesthouse on the Nouveau Kiskeya property.

- 17 ponds were dug providing 80,000 man-hours of work after the earthquake. These ponds now contain desperately-needed water for gardens and animals.

- 4000 families received a safe-water drinking system that prevented deaths during the cholera epidemic.

- a 14-room guesthouse was built in a remote part of NW Haiti that now serves as a spiritual training center for indigenous/local pastors.

- 40 local churches are united and working together to spread the Message of Jesus as a result of the indigenous Spiritual Warfare Campaign.

So the evidence adds up. Does this mean that when we respond to God's call there will always be measurable results? No, I don't think it always works that way, but for me, I can't explain the things I see in the rear-view mirror any other way. So was I called? Yes, I believe I was. Would I do it again? Yes, I believe I would.

Can a God Project Fail?

THIS HAD BEEN THE PRESSING QUESTION THAT ALMOST caused me to lose my faith in 2009. It wasn't until November 17, 2011, that I realized that my question contained a false assumption. It assumed that the project had failed. Though it may have failed by human standards, what I came to understand was that God's work should not be measured by human standards or human timetables.

Toward the end of 2009, I read A.W. Pink's commentary on the Beatitudes. Beatitude number eight seemed to shed an entirely new light on my experience:

> "Blessed are those who are persecuted
> because of righteousness
> for theirs is the kingdom of heaven."

Whenever I had thought about "the persecuted" in the past, my mind went intuitively to Christians who've been martyred over the past 2000 years. Since I had never been tortured or been required to give up something of great value because I was a Christian, I never considered myself in the category of the "persecuted".

However, as I read Pink's commentary, a light went on. I

was struck by his statements that "Things can go wrong even in God-ordained plans" and "Fiery trails are not evidence of God's disapproval." Those were my first indicators that human success was not necessarily the standard by which to evaluate God's work. Pink also helped me to understand that to be persecuted is a normal state of being a Christian and that persecution is a form of spiritual warfare.

Pink's book opened my eyes to the reality that during our efforts to develop the NK property, we actually had suffered persecution. Government officials had persecuted us because as Christians we had been committed to doing the right thing (righteousness). In this case that meant not participating in systemic corruption by paying bribes to government officials. Therefore, in reality, we were persecuted because we were Christians.

I now understand that from God's perspective the question is not whether our projects are successful or a failure, but whether we are sincerely seeking to do His will in everything we do. This truth is further reinforced by a quote from Dietrich Bonhoffer that a friend had given me two years earlier:

"The figure of the Crucified invalidates that success is the standard."

So the answer to my question is, *yes*, God-projects fail all the time if we are applying the yardstick of human success. That is because we are looking at them from the wrong perspective. If the Bible teaches us anything, it is that nothing God does fails. We may fail, but He assures us He can turn our apparent failures into great good. So, from God's perspective, He succeeds perfectly at everything He does.

Perhaps a better question is whether we were righteous in this undertaking. In other words, did we do the right thing? I think the answer, again, is *yes*. There is no question that we made mistakes, but we sought to be obedient each step of the way, as best we knew how. I now believe that the only thing for which we are responsible is to do the right thing. If we do the right thing, we are not responsible for the results.

Is It OK to Doubt God?

I GREW UP IN A WORLD WHERE FAITH WAS A 100% CONCEPT — all or nothing. If you had it, you went to heaven. If you didn't, you didn't. This is what we were taught at home, in school and in church. That scared me when what transpired in Haiti began shaking the core of my faith. But then, when doubt seemed to be overwhelming me, I picked up some books that began to give me hope. Through *Faith and Doubt*, by John Ortberg, *Soul Survivor* by Philip Yancy, *A Pastor's Journey from Faith to Doubt* by John Suk, and Fyodor Dostoevsky's *The Brothers Karamazov*, I began to understand that:

- Many Christians (especially thinking Christians) struggle with faith and doubt. While many doubt, few admit it because in most churches questioning conventional belief is regarded as heresy.

- Doubting is not the same as being an atheist or even an agnostic.

- Faith is a verb, not a noun. It isn't something we have; it is something we practice.

- If faith and doubt is a pendulum, as Yancy suggests, it makes sense that we might spend about 50% on each side.

- If faith was a 100% concept, growing in faith wouldn't make much sense.

I also learned that doubters are in good company: John the Baptist, Thomas the Apostle, Martin Luther, Blaise Pascal, Dwight Moody, Frederick Buechner, Philip Yancy, Fyodor Dostoevsky and Mother Teresa all experienced serious doubts.

So I recalibrated my faith and doubt meter. Instead of assuming that the norm is 100% faith and 0% doubt, I now accept the fact that I am having a good day when the faith side of the meter is above 50%.

I can now also look back and conclude that faith and doubt are not opposites. Not only are they not contradictory, in an unconventional way, God used my doubts to strengthen my faith.

PRACTICAL
REFLECTIONS

Practical Lessons Learned

*Development Work
Do's and Don'ts*

The Bottom Line

Discussion Questions

Conclusion

Practical Lessons Learned

THE FOLLOWING LESSONS RESULTED FROM TEN YEARS OF experience trying to alleviate poverty in Haiti. While you may not agree with all of my observations, it is my hope that they will stimulate constructive and enlightening conversations that can be used to improve the lives of people around the world. I also hope that sharing these hard-won lessons will help others avoid making the mistakes that I made.

1. Doing *anything* in an underdeveloped country is difficult.

This may seem obvious but it is surprisingly easy to skip over this reality in the excitement of trying to make a difference somewhere in the world. It is clearly something I did not pay enough attention to and consistently minimized in my sincere desire to help the people of Haiti.

The following is a partial list of reasons why it is so much more difficult to do almost any kind of work in an underdeveloped country:

- there will be physical *distance* between you and the people you are trying to help. Working from a distance is always more difficult than doing that same thing locally.

144

- there will probably be *language differences.*
  Communicating through third parties complicates
  the communication process significantly.

- there will certainly be *cultural* differences. These can lead
  to huge misunderstandings. Because this is such a crucial
  issue, I will address cultural issues more thoroughly later.

- underdeveloped countries typically do not have
  the infrastructure that we are used to. The utility
  infrastructure we take for granted for production and
  manufacturing either does not exist or it is extremely
  undependable. The transportation system is typically in
  poor condition. In addition, the justice infrastructure is
  frequently either non-existent or corrupt.

These difficulties do not mean that we should stop working with people in underdeveloped countries. But they do suggest that we take the time to understand and seriously consider the unique difficulties of starting or growing a business in an underdeveloped country.

Before going to Haiti I had been involved in starting seven businesses in the United States. All of them had been successful. As it turned out, that experience was not adequate preparation for starting a successful business in Haiti. I wish I had appreciated how unprepared I was and how much I did not know.

Cross-cultural work is the classic scenario Proverbs alludes to when it suggests that "plans fail for lack of counsel, but with many advisers they succeed." Most of us launch out not knowing how desperately we need counsel from those who have traveled a similar journey before us. Ideally, we should seek counselors who have spent enough time in our country of choice to lead the way and to protect us from the inevitable pitfalls and land mines we will come across along the way.

2. Do not do anything in an underdeveloped country that you wouldn't do in your own back yard.

I don't know why, but North Americans tend to believe that they can do anything anywhere. I know I certainly did. This level of confidence can be a real strength — it can also be a huge problem.

This tendency toward over-confidence leads people who have no experience in, let's say, commercial fishing or raising fish, to assume they can go to an underdeveloped country to "teach" people how to start a fish farm. I suspect that this is due to the gross disparity of resources that results in the presumption that we as "wealthy" North Americans know better than the "poor people" in the nation we have come to help. In reality, wealth does not necessarily convey experience, wisdom or superior insight.

While we bear much of the responsibility for creating these unrealistic expectations, I have also noticed that the people we are trying to help tend to reinforce them. Unconscious pressure can be placed on those of us with altruistic motives when we are asked for help that we are not really qualified to give. In Ecuador, I was asked to come to a meeting to teach farmers how to grow tomatoes in greenhouses. I have no idea how to grow tomatoes in greenhouses. When

I told the Ecuadorians that I didn't know how to grow tomatoes in greenhouses they seemed surprised. Apparently, their assumption was that North Americans can provide advice on any subject that relates directly or indirectly to making money. The psychological power our wealth gives us over the poor is something we should never ignore, for it can set up both parties for cruel disappointment.

As you look at doing something in an underdeveloped country, I would suggest you start by limiting yourself to something at which you are really good. Then you need to determine whether the country you're interested in could benefit from that skill. For example, if your expertise is in setting up irrigation systems there are two preliminary questions I would encourage you to ask: is there a need in your country of choice for that type of expertise? And, will the increase in productivity cover the cost of installation? If the answer to both of these questions is yes, taking a trip to explore the possibility of helping poor farmers with such systems might not be a bad idea. However, if on the other hand, you are an accountant, starting a farm in an underdeveloped country is probably not a good idea. The lesson is deceptively simple: operate in your area of giftedness.

3. Do not assume that you have solutions for problems in another culture.

Start with this counter-intuitive conviction: you probably do not even understand the problem much less its solution. This is especially true if you do not have a thorough understanding of the country's culture. It is interesting to me that North Americans accept the fact that when traveling to a country where they do not speak English a language translator is important. But what seems to be almost completely ignored by those interested in doing "business as mission" in a foreign context is the vital necessity of a cultural translator. This is a unique individual who can translate both what is being done and what is being said into your cultural context. While everyone intuitively understands that a language translator needs to know both languages, it is not as self-evident that a cultural translator needs to understand not only both languages but also both cultures.

I haven't met too many people who meet the qualifications for this crucial role. I believe that to be truly helpful in this capacity, this person has to have lived in and experienced both cultures for at least ten years.

Where do you find a cultural translator? Unfortunately they are not listed in the Yellow Pages. One option is to find someone from your culture who has lived in the other culture for at least ten years. Another source is to find a native of that country who has spent at least ten years in your culture. What cannot be overstated is that you need to find at least one cultural translator, and more than one if possible, and they should be part of your team.

4. Cross-cultural work is not for everyone.

Cross-cultural work is tough! This is true even if you decide to work in Philadelphia's inner-city, in Appalachia, on a Native American Reservation in North Dakota, or in the inner city of your own town. However, international cross-cultural work is incrementally more difficult. Culture is the wiring that impacts how people think and directs what people do. If you do not understand why a person does what he does it is almost impossible to truly help them. To understand someone who thinks differently than you do requires patience, and to have a positive impact in a context that is foreign to you demands humility. You cannot come in with the arrogant assumption that you know exactly what the problem is and how to resolve it. The truth of it is that if you have difficulty listening to and learning from others, you should strongly consider staying home.

I can almost guarantee that North American Type-A personalities, who expect a certain work ethic and measurable results in relatively short order, will get frustrated in cross-cultural work. In addition, in some underdeveloped countries, corruption is so pervasive that blatant dishonesty impacts everyone and everything at every level.

In Haiti, for example, it is conventional wisdom that a government job, at any level, is a license to steal. This reality is even supported by a Haitian proverb: "Stealing from the government isn't stealing." If your personality makes it impossible to deal graciously with these realities, you may need to accept the fact that cross-cultural work is not for you.

5. Poverty is not just a money problem.

Addressing the needs of the poor is hard, complicated work that frequently requires systemic changes in the way the poor do things and in the way their country operates. Typically, an influx of money and/or expertise by itself does not solve the problem. Note the billions of dollars and man-hours the international community has invested in underdeveloped countries over the years, frequently with minimal results. These efforts may be successful in improving the lives of a few people but widespread poverty requires systemic change and systemic change can only come from within.

6. Increased Productivity is the only Cure for Poverty.

From a practical perspective, the only way for someone to improve their standard of living is for them to increase their productivity. This is true for an individual and it is true for a country. To help people increase their productivity, the focus needs to be on skill training and creating access to the tools of productivity: capital, equipment, facilities, etc. However, the standard for determining whether the investment is worthwhile is whether it can be repaid as a result of the increased productivity. Therefore, any work designed to increase the standard of living should ultimately be self-funding.

7. A Free Market Economy is essential to the elimination of Poverty

The following notes were strongly influenced by *The Cure for Poverty: It's the Free Market: History's Greatest Invention*. Meyer E Herbert, Storm King Press. Kindle Edition.

Helping people increase their standard of living is extremely difficult in situations where the country's government is unwilling or unable to promote a free market economy. A free market economy includes:

- documented private property rights that are protected by a court of law,
- enforcement of civil law,
- taxation with enforcement,
- competent regulation without corruption,
- protection for its citizens (primarily from each other),
- provision of infrastructure (roads, ports, airports, utilities, schools),

and

- a culture of trust.

Countries that are not willing or not able to provide a free market economy will not attract the investment capital needed to grow an economy and the jobs that come with it. During the past two decades a number of countries that understood the necessity of a free market economy have proven this point. As a result, between 50 and 100 million people per year worldwide, have emerged from poverty as a result of their governments realizing that the best way to promote economic growth was to eliminate the obstacles to a free market economy. This means that during the last 20 years, at least one billion people have emerged from poverty whereas I know of no country where productivity, jobs and the standard of living were significantly improved through the philanthropic efforts of NGOs.

Meyer also points out that because a free market economy promotes job creation and the consequent increase of income for its people, it also generates tax revenue for the government to do what only the government can do. Therefore an important key to breaking the cycle of poverty is a free market economy.

Although Haiti is considered to be a democracy it does not meet the definition of a free market economy by the above standards.

The current reality in Haiti is that:

- property-rights documentation is poor.
- law enforcement is sparse and often corrupt.
- tax evasion is normal.
- regulators are understaffed and frequently incompetent and corrupt.
- justice systems are erratic and corrupt.
- infrastructure is weak and undependable.

Until the Haitian Government is ready, willing and able to implement the standards of a free market economy, in my opinion, little will change.

8. The absence of a foundation of moral values contributes to poverty.

Regardless of one's opinion of the current moral values of the West, most people would not deny that economic progress in the West was fostered by an underpinning of Judeo-Christian values:

- the Golden Rule,
- respect for one's neighbor,
- do the right thing,

- be a Good Samaritan,
- sacrificial giving,
- self discipline,
- self respect,
- respect for leaders,
- individual responsibility,
- gratitude,
- compassion.

Judeo Christian values based on the Hebrew and the Christian Bible have had a tremendous influence on establishing the moral code in the West. Anthropologists have demonstrated that these values have continued to have a positive influence on commerce even as belief in the religions that promulgated these values has waned.

9. Religion has a major impact on culture.

"Animism is a dominant religion in many underdeveloped countries. Animism encompasses the beliefs that there is no separation between the spiritual and physical (or material) worlds, and that souls or spirits exist, not only in humans, but also in animals, plants, rocks, natural phenomena such as thunder, geographic features such as mountains or rivers, or other entities of the natural environment." (Wikipedia). In Haiti the dominant religion is voodoo. Voodoo is "a spirit religion, that likely evolved from ancient traditions of ancestor worship and animism." (Brian Handwerk, *National Geographic News.*) Animism and voodoo tend to keep people in a condition of dependency because their religion suggests that the spirits control everything. As a result, the people conclude that they have no control over anything, including their own destiny. The religion of Haiti thus breeds passivity and hopelessness, and destroys belief in the power of personal agency.

10. Not all "poor" people need our help.

Because of our historically, high income levels in North America, it isn't hard to find comparatively poor people all over the world. However, the average standard of living in the United States should not be the standard for assessing international poverty. The Bible says that if you have food, shelter and clothing you should be content. Because of its availability today, we might want to add clean water, basic healthcare and basic education to the Biblical standard. It wasn't too long ago that most people in the world, including the United States, didn't have much more than these basic elements. The Biblical standard for the poor that we are called to help are the oppressed, the vulnerable and the helpless. As we look around us we may want to keep that Biblical standard in mind instead of rushing in to help anyone who has less money than we do.

11. Do things with people not for people.

In a *relief* situation we frequently need to do things for people. After all, relief is frequently a matter of life or death. In a *development* situation it is important that we always do things *with* the people who will benefit. The approach of doing things with the people who will benefit starts even before you decide what you are going to do. You need to talk with those you want to help to really understand their needs and what resources they may have to address those needs. The best-case scenario is that in the process of discussing their needs, you will mutually discover what they could do to improve their situation. If that isn't possible, look for creative ways that you could work together in partnership to address their need. The worst-case scenario is when you do all the work and/or provide all the money. That rarely works because the "help" you are bringing will create dependency. A unilateral infusion of money and expertise, unfortunately, robs the recipients of dignity and a sense of personal significance. So, whatever you do, make sure that the people you are trying to help have "skin in the game".

12. There are dark sides to development work.

(a) Earlier in this section I suggested that development work was not for amateurs. One of the reasons is that there are frequently local people in underdeveloped countries who might take advantage of you as an amateur. Many of these people work the system for their own benefit and to make things even more complicated, some of these people call themselves "pastors". This is an unfortunate reality since Christians in the West tend to respect and trust a Pastor. Needless to say, when an amateur teams up with a professional it is not hard to imagine who is going to win.

(b) I have learned that in development work there is a reluctance to hold people accountable because we don't want to be too harsh. After all, these people have so many problems we do not want to add to them. However, not requiring accountability is a mistake. Encouraging people to honor their commitments is actually doing them a favor. Hopefully they will learn that taking accountability for their actions will help them get from where they are to where they want to be.

(c) I have also learned that in development work it is very easy to give people too much too soon. One of the reasons we tend to give too much too fast is that our paradigm and our scales are different. I remember when a Haitian businessman asked me for a loan of $20,000. I agreed to loan him half of that amount. I later learned that $10,000 was much more than he had ever seen and he was not prepared to manage that much money. As a result he was not able to pay off the entire loan. Three years later he sent me a note admitting the shame that resulted from his inability to repay the loan. Even though I told him the loan balance was forgiven, the consequence of this loan may have been harder on him than it was on me.

(d) The fact that development work can take years and sometimes generations sets the stage for three unintended negative consequences: minimal accountability for results on the part of the development organization; unclear definition of the finish line; and local dependency on the presence of the development organizations as their work becomes ingrained into the economy of the country.

13. Culture matters!

Every people group has their own culture. This is true in North America and around the world. Culture explains why people groups do what they do, think the way they think and believe what they believe. If you are involved in cross-cultural work and if you do not understand the culture you are working in, you will be continuously confused, frustrated and disappointed. Inevitably, you will become resentful, angry and maybe even quit as I was tempted to do after only three years into my journey.

The following are some of the cultural obstacles to job creation in Haiti that I wish I had understood when I began:

- Risk is discouraged rather than encouraged.
- Success is resented rather than celebrated.
- Obstacles are proof that progress is impossible.
- Foreigners are either viewed with deep suspicion or are idolized as the exclusive source of economic salvation.
- The future is considered to be hopeless rather than filled with promise and opportunity.
- Relationships are governed by suspicion, distrust and fear.
- Corruption is expected from institutions, officials and leaders.
- Initiative and responsibility are resisted by pervasive fatalistic beliefs.
- Passivity rather than active involvement is the primary political/economic posture.
- Bureaucratic procedure is more important than efficient results.
- Circumstances rather than time controls plans and agendas.

- Foreigners and even the Diaspora are viewed as donors not partners.
- Cooperation is a threat to individual power rather than a means for mutual success.
- Deception and dishonesty are regarded as virtue not vice.

14. For-profit business is difficult in underdeveloped countries!

Everyone in the non-profit "poverty-elimination business" tends to affirm the concept that for-profit business and the jobs it creates are the solution to poverty. However, most people do not understand how difficult it is to start a successful business anywhere, even in highly developed cultures. The reality is that 80% of businesses *in the United States* fail within 5 years! Consider the likelihood of success in an underdeveloped country that does not have the infrastructure to support a business enterprise and where the competition sometimes succeeds not on efficiency and quality but on advantages obtained through the payment of bribes.

15. The dilemma of Partnership.

When working in a foreign culture most of us would agree that to accomplish anything significant we need local partners who can help us navigate unknown territory. However, the very concept of partnership implies equality: equality of investment, equality of contribution, equality of potential gain, and equality of potential loss. Unless your in-country partners truly meet this definition you are not equal partners.

As a result, your in-country friends may go along with whatever you propose, especially if you are providing the money. Therefore a true partnership model is very difficult to achieve but nevertheless very important. Partners need to need each other.

It is very difficult to set up a partnership of equals in a cross-cultural situation especially if you are the one bringing the money and the expertise because money and expertise tend to control. The only way that I have found to balance the partnership scale is to trust your partner enough to give them control over the success or failure of the project. You can help set the goals and the boundaries and the benchmarks but you have to be willing to surrender control. The right partner will know a lot more about how to do things successfully in their culture and environment than you do. Giving up control is a risky proposition but unless your partner contributes as much as you do and has as much to lose as you do, you are not partners.

Development Work
Do's and Don'ts

1. Don't go it alone.

If there are others who have gone before you, learn from them. If there are others who have similar interests, create a team. If there are other organizations addressing similar problems, learn from them and if possible partner with them. Development work is not for amateurs.

2. Find knowledgeable partners who you like and trust.

North American entrepreneurs tend to be accustomed to calling the shots. That may work in a context where you know the rules but it rarely works where the rules are very different, or, worse, where you do not even know what they are.

Any attempt to create solutions to problems in underdeveloped countries must include knowledgeable indigenous people whether they live in that country or in that country's Diaspora, as well as North Americans with experience in that country. In other words, create a cross-cultural team of experienced people and have the grace to submit to their superior knowledge base.

Be very careful in selecting your indigenous partners. Almost everyone in underdeveloped countries understands that friendship and partnership with a North American increases their personal prestige and their ability to make money. Great discernment is needed to select those who have a genuine interest in serving others rather than advancing themselves. Test their responsibility and integrity by degrees knowing that at the end of the day you must be able to trust them implicitly. Also, make sure they actually have the competencies they claim and the ones you actually need, otherwise you will be in the unfortunate predicament of the blind leading the blind. Good intentions are not good enough!

3. Triangulate all information.

As you develop friendships, relationships and partnerships with local people it is important that you do not rely on just one person as your information source. You need to find multiple, preferably unrelated, sources to verify what you are being told before you decide whether you can help and the best way to do so.

4. Understand where the power is.

In most underdeveloped countries, even in countries that are theoretically democracies, power is in the hands of the elite. Unfortunately, that is frequently one of the root causes of that country's poverty. This privileged minority typically does not have the best interest of the people at heart, just as European colonial powers did not have the best interest of the native people in mind.

The Haitian elite publically disparages the masses who

live in the countryside by referring to them as "peasants." The resistance of this entrenched, educated, and self-interested powerbase is one of the biggest obstacles to systemic change. Machiavelli said "The reason there will be no change is because the people who stand to lose from change have all the power and the people who stand to gain from change have none of the power." If Machiavelli is right we can conclude that nothing will change until the change agents benefit from the change.

5. Focus on people not projects.

It is very easy to get excited about a project. It is also very easy to let its demands cause you to lose your focus on the people impacted by it. All projects are first and foremost about the people.

6. Find an import and replace it.

The dream of many craftsmen in underdeveloped countries is to export their product to the West; after all, that is where the money is. If that works, that is great. However, the reality is that many of these products are not ready for prime time. In addition, export requires a significant distribution chain of warehousing, transportation and shipping, and involves complex import/export legal issues, not to mention wholesale and retail sales distribution channels. Even with these elements in place we can't assume that the local product will be competitive in the international marketplace.

By focusing on international export, there may be an in-country market that is being overlooked. This is what is behind the idea of finding an import and replacing it with a local substitute.

On my first trip to Haiti I visited my friend Ernso's grocery store. After scanning the shelves for a while it appeared to me that 80% of the items in his grocery store were imported from the Dominican Republic and other countries. Relatively simple products like beans, ketchup, honey and eggs were being brought in from the outside. It seemed to me then and it seems to me now that the first market for local productivity should be the local market.

7. Start small.

North Americans tend to think big. That's fine, but starting big in an environment that you probably do not understand is generally not a good idea. In addition, it is also virtually guaranteed to overwhelm the people you are trying to help. Begin small and work your way up. Most successful businesses start small. This is even true in North America. However, the needs in underdeveloped countries are so massive that there is a tremendous temptation to start something much larger than you should. The bigger you start, the bigger the mistakes that you will make. And the more damage you may cause.

Big projects also require big changes among those you wish to help. Don't assume that they are able or willing to make large radical adjustments to accommodate your proposed big changes. As a wise friend with lengthy experience in Haiti told me, "Poor people live on the edge and can not afford to take big risks." (Neil Van Dine, Haiti Outreach.)

It is better to start small, focus on early success and build on that success. This requires patience, a commodity in short supply among most North Americans anxious to meet the needs of the poor. I remember having a discussion with a Haitian friend. He is smart and educated. Economically, he is in his country's top 10%. As we were discussing the state of Haiti he said to me, "Ted, you need to understand that our country is only 200 years old." He was totally serious. Perhaps I should have taken his comment more seriously.

8. Start with the end in mind.

I will admit, this one is really difficult! We are problem solvers. Once we find people who we want to help, the last thing we want to think about is leaving them. However, we need to have an exit strategy right from the start. We need to define when the task will be finished. If we don't do that upfront and if all of the parties do not understand and agree on when the project will be finished, we have unwittingly set up a scenario that could end badly or worse, never end.

If we stay too long because we do not have a pre-defined exit strategy we will get frustrated. Leaving without properly preparing the people we are working with will result in their disappointment and resentment because they will feel abandoned. Therefore it is critical that we start with the end in mind. Picturing what you consider as a successful outcome will help define what needs to be done and how to do it as well as provide a benchmark to help you identify your progress.

9. Understand the self-image of the people you are trying to help.

Most people in underdeveloped countries are poor. Poor

people tend to believe that they are inferior. As a result they do not believe that they can fix their own problems. This fosters dependency. In contrast, most North Americans are rich. Rich people feel superior. This leads to pride. It also leads to thinking that we have solutions to problems we don't even understand.

A major contributor to economic poverty is poverty of spirit, which results from a loss of faith in oneself. Children, both in the West and in underdeveloped countries, want to become astronauts and doctors or famous sports and entertainment figures, and they have complete confidence that this is possible. However, as children in the underdeveloped world grow older their innate optimism is frequently squashed by the realities of their life. Before long their dreams disappear as they begin to concentrate on simple survival and they join the ranks of adults who also came to believe that "nothing good can happen in our country."

10. Treat the problem not the symptom.

Those of us who live in North America see an endless number of headlines in newspapers and fund raising letters describing horrible situations around the world. Frequently, our impulse is to respond, either personally or financially. Although well intentioned, that impulsive response can result in treating the symptom rather than the real problem. A classic example of this situation might be a headline screaming "Babies dying for lack of clean water." Our response might be to help dig a well. That may temporarily solve the problem but upon further investigation you may discover that this is the third well that is being dug in this village. The real problem, it turns out, is that the villagers have not been challenged to put any sweat equity into their water source and have never been taught how to maintain it. So in this case the real cause of the problem was the lack of partnership with the villagers.

11. Understand the difference between relief and development.

Relief is keeping people in crisis alive and tending to their basic, immediate needs. Development is moving people in need from the first rung of the economic ladder to the second rung. Relief is temporary. Development is long-term. Relief will probably include hand-outs. Development is providing a hand-up.

Since the rules for each are completely different, it is essential that you understand whether you need to employ a relief or a development model with your project. Relief is frequently a matter of life or death. Development is a long-term effort to improve people's standard of living and usually focuses more on training than on providing the basics of life. (Reading *When Helping Hurts*, an excellent book written by Brian Fikkert and Steve Corbett, fostered much of my understanding about the crucial difference between relief and development. I highly recommend it.)

12. Beware of what you bring into an underdeveloped country!

When we become aware of "needs" in an underdeveloped country our tendency is to fill shipping containers with the items we think they lack, be it food, water, clothing, shoes, home construction material or healthcare products, and ship it to those in "need." Then, when it arrives, and assuming it is released from customs, we distribute the contents at no cost.

Let's examine three economic consequences of this "act of mercy".

(a) Everything we bring into a country has the potential of negatively impacting the local economy, businesses, their owners and their employees!

- if we bring in food we harm farmers, food resellers and others in the food industry,
- if we bring in water we harm people who earn their living in the water industry,
- if we bring in clothing we harm people who earn their living in the textile industry,
- if we bring in home construction material we harm people who earn their living in the home building industry,
- if we bring in healthcare products we harm people in the pharmaceutical industry.

Everything we bring into a country competes with local productivity and local jobs.

(b) Giving resources away for free can destroy local businesses. No business can compete with FREE! Anytime we bring in stuff and give it away or charge less than the local market price, *we are destroying a tiny part of the local economy*.

We tend to assume that poor people do not have any money. Therefore we give them stuff at no cost. Our assumption may not necessarily be true. The fact that cell phones are ubiquitous in many underdeveloped countries, even among very poor people, proves that even the very poor have some money. Although their bank account might be a goat, a pig or a cow, many have some money and will spend it on things that they value. In the case of Haiti, I am not aware of any NGO that brings free cell phones, yet half of the population owns one.

(c) When we give stuff away for free we destroy the self-worth and the dignity of the people we are trying to help. It is extremely hard to work among the poor without creating entitlement and dependency. Too frequently, our tendency to rush in with arms full of gifts creates dependency that short-circuits the personal initiative and responsibility that are absolutely essential to breaking the cycle of poverty. As Chuck Roost, the Founder of International Steward says: "Dependency soon evolves into entitlement and entitlement destroys. Dependency kills initiative and robs the people of their future."

Bottom line: be aware of the destructive consequences that may result from our sincere desire to help the poor. Before bringing anything, ask yourself the following questions:

- is whatever I want to bring really necessary? If the answer is no; don't!

- can I buy that item or service in country? If the answer is yes; buy local!

- can the beneficiary contribute at least a part of the cost? If the item has perceived value, the answer is usually yes. If it is no, you may want to seriously question if it is needed.

13. Before you invest, investigate.

Before you invest yourself in a relief or a development project, get the facts and separate the "facts" from the story. There are an endless number of heart-breaking stories used to raise money. There are an equal number of "apparent success" stories that are used for the same purpose. Before investing in a development project, ask lots of questions. At minimum you should be able to answer each of the following critical questions:

- What is the problem?
- What is the solution?
- Who will be the beneficiaries?
- Who will be responsible for solving the problem?
- What will be the cost of solving the problem?
- What will be the payback of solving the problem?
- What is your exit strategy?

(For additional detail on sub-questions in these categories, please see "Seven Critical Questions" in the Appendix.)

It is very easy to get excited about a project that will help the poor. It all seems so simple and the payoffs appear to be huge: malaria nets cut the frequency of malaria in half, fresh water wells will significantly reduce the death rate of little children, a fish pond can give hundreds of people and children the protein that will allow them to grow strong bones. What can be so hard about starting a fishpond? And so it goes.

I, too, got caught in that trap many times; the last time

was in 2010. We had a water source that could literally pro-
duce one million gallons of water per day and we had farmers downhill from the wellhead whose crops were failing for
lack of water. In addition, I had a friend who is one of the
world's experts on drip irrigation. Though the opportunity
was compelling and the solution seemed straightforward,
we eventually learned that the project would never become
self-supporting. As a result we had no choice but to table the
project, to our disappointment and to that of the local farmers. However, we did learn a valuable lesson. We learned that
before starting a project it is necessary to ask a lot of questions. The questions listed above and further detailed in the
appendix were a result of that process. If you are going to
start a project in unfamiliar territory, I would encourage you
to ask yourself these questions before you get too far into the
process.

14. Don't do for others what they can do for themselves.

Bringing a North American team to build homes, schools
or churches to a country with 80% unemployment is not a
good idea. It would be better to find local people who know
how to build homes, and then, in addition, employ untrained
local people to help the local homebuilders. This approach
will probably be much less expensive plus it will result in skill
learning and income opportunities for the people you want
to help and it treats them with dignity. It applies to almost
everything you may want to do for others, including medical care. After the 2010 earthquake in Haiti there were so

many international medical workers providing free medical services in Haiti that some of the Haitian medical workers moved to Montreal in order to be able to earn a living. Obviously, Haiti needed medical help, but some of the NGO's broke the cardinal rule of first making sure to respect the local people who are able to do what we do and earn their living doing it. No one can compete with free.

The Bottom Line

ADMITTEDLY, THE LESSONS I LEARNED AND SPELLED OUT above might be enough to scare you off from helping the poor. That was not my intent in writing this book. I honestly believe that if I knew then what I know now I would still have followed the call to Haiti, but would have done a lot of things differently. As I think back about my journey I ask myself what was the most important lesson I learned that ultimately made the biggest personal impact? The answer is wrapped up in a concept known as **Subsidiarity**. I first heard that word in 2007 from my friends at the Acton Institute (Acton.org) but it took several years for its significance to sink in. As indicated on one of the Acton websites (povertycure.org/issues) its thesis is that "an issue or problem should be dealt with by the people who are closest to it...." This is a simple but profound idea.

Simply stated, subsidiarity suggests that when my neighbor has a problem I am in the best position to help. This is true in my neighborhood and it is true around the world. When we in the West rush in to solve problems halfway around the world we violate the principle of subsidiarity and in the process obviate the responsibility of local neighbors, relatives and governments who will understand the problem and the solution to the problem much better than we do.

Does this mean that we do not have a responsibility to help people who live far from us? Of course we do. But we need to be careful how we exercise that responsibility. If we are aware of a need we should look for honorable people, preferably indigenous, who are proximately closer to the need and equipped to address it. We should then help these people or that organization in any way that we can to help their neighbors. Of course we have to do our homework to verify that they are credible, honest and competent. When we apply this approach there may even be times that we decide to stay out of the way. If that happens, we can look for needs that are closer to home, needs that we are in a better position to understand, and in a better position to help without hurting.

In the case of Haiti, only Haitians can solve Haiti's problems. All NGO and international aid efforts should be secondary and temporary. If the international community stays too long they will own the problem and possibly make it worse by fostering a victim or entitlement mentality. Today this is already effectively true in Haiti, which has become known as the Republic of NGO's. The West cannot "fix" Haiti or any other underdeveloped country in the world. History will defend that statement. The West should stop wasting money attempting the impossible.

If the Government of Haiti or any other underdeveloped country in the world would start doing what governments are supposed to do they would not need the "help" that is being offered by the international community. In addition, anyone in the West who wants to help alleviate poverty needs to understand the following to avoid doing more harm than good:

- the concept of subsidiarity and the dangers of creating dependence.
- that giving away goods and services usually destroys a tiny part of the local economy in the country we are trying to help.
- that every project controlled and managed by the West undermines the abilities of local people.

Back in 2004, when we were led to start the Rescue One Children's ministry, I had never heard of the concept of subsidiarity. However, ironically, as it turned out, Rescue One may have turned out to be an ultimate example of this principle at work:

- my wife Jan and I had been made aware of the need to rescue children from the restavec system (child slavery), by a Haitian national.
- we hired a Haitian national to direct our efforts to rescue children.
- we strongly encouraged a partnership between our Haitian Director and local Haitian churches.
- we admitted that we did not know how to rescue children and told our Haitian partners that they needed to figure out how to do it.
- we placed the responsibility for making the major decisions on our indigenous partners.

- we agreed to match the financial investment of the Haitian churches on a sliding scale basis so that they would have immediate ownership in the initiative and would gradually contribute more and we would contribute less.

The Rescue One initiative is now in it's ninth year and children who might not have gone to school at all are now graduating from High School. (For more information about Rescue One, please see www.rescue-one.org)

Discussion Questions

MY PREFERRED WAY OF LEARNING IS TO IDENTIFY QUES-
tions, try to find answers and then discuss them with others.
If you would like to wrestle with some of the issues I thought
about in the last ten years I would suggest that you think
about the following questions and then discuss them with
others. My hope is that by addressing them you will develop
a better understanding of current poverty issues and be able
to better discern what it is that God wants you to do to be a
light to the world.

1. Who are the poor of the 21st Century?

2. Why are the poor poor?

3. What is the Biblical basis for helping the poor?

4. What is our responsibility, as Christians, to the poor?

5. What is the best way to help the poor?

6. What are the responsibilities of the poor while they are
   being helped?

7. What is the Biblical basis for relief work (disaster response)? This could be a disaster in a local family or a disaster in some region of the world.

8. Why is cross-cultural work so difficult?

9. Why is it that North Americans think they can go almost anywhere in the world and solve other people's problems?

10. Since our culture and our religious practices are as foreign to people in other countries and other cultures as their culture and religion is to us, is it naïve to assume that Western Christians can have much impact on a short-term mission trip to a foreign culture?

11. Why do people, including Christians, respond much more spontaneously and generously to natural disasters than to long-term development work or to the work of sharing the message of Jesus?

12. Assuming it is true that the definition of "economic development" is to move people from the first rung of the economic ladder to the second rung what is the Biblical basis for "economic development"?

13. When is development work finished?

14. Given the complexity and difficulty of creating jobs as a poverty solution, what is the best way for churches to participate in job creation as one of their mission goals?

15. The Bible says that if you have food, shelter and clothing you should be content. There are clearly people in our world who do not have these three basic things. However, we in the West feel compelled to help the "poor" who have all these things and a whole lot more (think micro waves, air-conditioning, and 42" television sets). Have we broadened the category of the poor too much?

16. Development organizations tend to want to address problems in a wide variety of countries, twenty or thirty is not unusual. Given the complexity and profound impact of culture, should development organizations specialize
in fewer countries?

17. Most poverty is a result of systemic problems. What is the best way to address socially, culturally and religiously entrenched systemic problems?

18. It's been said that we should be looking at the causes of wealth rather than the causes of poverty. Do you agree?

19. Haitians are proud of their country. It used to be and in many places still is a nation of great beauty. However, development agencies tend to use stories and pictures of sad children and garbage-laden streams and rivers to raise money. This obviously has a negative influence on the international image of the country. Is that fair?

20. How should the concept of subsidiarity impact what we do and how we do it as we follow the Biblical mandate to love mercy?

21. Henri Nouwen, a Catholic priest and a prolific author who spent a lot of time with the poor in South America, discovered a paradox. The poor and the oppressed, especially in the underdeveloped world, have a more profound sense of God's love and are happier than we Westerners who live materially privileged lives. Yet we seem to operate from the premise that we can help the poor by giving them material goods. Are we Westerners too anxious to materially "enrich" the poor?

Conclusion

THIS STORY IS NOT FINISHED. IT IS A WORK IN PROCESS because both Nouveau Kiskeya and I are a work in process. I am not sure how God wants to use Nouveau Kiskeya but He is certainly capable of resurrecting it. I also do not know how He wants to use me but I am open. I certainly have not learned everything there is to know about the causes of poverty and I am open to learning more. Perhaps you can help. I hope that this book and its website (www.demonsofpoverty .com) will stimulate a conversation from which we can all continue to learn. If it does, the process of writing this book will have been worthwhile.

APPENDICES

The Remove Curses Prayer

Seven Critical Questions

The Remove Curses Prayer

LORD, OUR GOD, WE DECIDE TODAY TO FULLY OBEY YOU and carefully follow all the commands you give us.

We renounce and denounce the making of sacrifices and services to other gods, we renounce and denounce the practices of divination or sorcery, we renounce and denounce the practices of interpreting omens, we renounce and denounce the practices of engaging in witchcraft, we renounce and denounce the practices of casting spells, we renounce and denounce the practices of medium or spiritist, we renounce and denounce the practices of consulting the dead because, LORD, you detest anyone who does these things.

Yes, LORD, because we decide to fully obey you and carefully follow all the commands you, our God, give us, here are the blessings we are asking you to pour on us according to your promise:

LORD, bless us everywhere we are. Bless our children. Bless the crops of our land and the young of our livestock, the calves of our herds and the lambs of our flocks. Bless all our activities. Bless us in every thing that we do. Bless us when we come in and bless us when we go out.

LORD, grant that all enemies who rise up against us will

be defeated before us. Bless us at all times. Bless our barns; bless everything we put our hand to. Bless us right here, in the region where you, our God, have placed us.

LORD, our God, because we decide to keep your commands and walk in obedience to you, cause our region to become a holy place, living a holy life for you, LORD, our God.

LORD, our God, cause all the peoples on earth to see that you have called our region to bear your name. Cause them to respect us.

LORD, grant us abundant prosperity, bless the fruit of our womb, the young of our livestock and the crops of our ground, right here in the region where you, LORD, our God, have placed us.

LORD, open the heavens, the storehouse of your bounty, to send rain on our region in season and to bless all the work of our hands. Cause us to always be able to lend to others. Cause that we never have to borrow from anyone. Make us the head and never the tail. Cause us to always be at the top and never at the bottom because, LORD, we pay attention to your commands and we decide this day to carefully follow them.

LORD, because we decide to not turn aside, to the right or to the left, from any of the commands you give us, to not follow other gods and serve them, we ask you to remove the following curses from us:

The curses that are on us everywhere we are; the curses that are on our children, on our crops, on the calves of our herds and the lambs of our flocks.

Please, LORD, remove all those curses that are upon us in everything we put our hand to, when we come in and when we go out.

In the name of Jesus Christ, your son

Amen!

Prepared by PASTOR ROBERT ULYSSE (2010)

Seven Critical Questions

SEVEN ESSENTIAL QUESTIONS THAT MUST BE ANSWERED before starting a *Development Project*: (If this is a relief project, these questions may not apply.)

1. The Problem

- What is the problem?

- Why does the problem exist?

- What will happen if the problem is not solved?

- Who is the closest (physically and relationally) to being able to solve it?

- What are the people who are experiencing the problem doing to solve it?

- Is your help necessary to solve the problem?

2. The Solution

- What is the proposed solution?

- What is the best approach to solving the problem?

- Will the solution be sustainable?

- What will define success?

- Is the project capable of producing the results anticipated by all the parties?
- Is this project technically possible in the targeted community?
- How long will it take for the project to become self-sustaining?
- If expertise is needed, who will provide it?

3. The Beneficiaries

- Who will be the beneficiaries that will benefit from this project?
- How many potential beneficiaries are there?
- Can the beneficiaries pay some or all of the cost?
- Did the beneficiaries request this project?
  Do they want it?
- Are the beneficiaries involved in the process of solving the problem?
- What are the beneficiaries' responsibilities?
- Are the beneficiaries willing and able to fulfill their responsibilities?
- Is this project capitalizing on the assets the beneficiaries already have?
- What are the positive and negative consequences of this project on the beneficiaries and their community?
- Will this project favor some people over others?
- Will this project create dependency or entitlement?

4. The Manager

- Who will manage the process of solving the problem?
- What will be the manager's specific responsibilities?
- Is the manager qualified?
- Does the manager have a successful track record with projects of this nature?
- Do you like and trust the manager?
- Does the manager have a vested interest in making the project successful?
- Is the manager qualified, competent, and culturally aware?
- Are there other organizations that serve this need in the area or in the country? Can you partner with them?

5. The Cost

- What will be the cost of solving the problem?
- Is the project economically viable in view of startup cost, operating costs and maintenance costs?
- Does it make sense to spend this much money on solving this problem?
- If investment is needed, where will the money come from and can you raise it?
- How much of the cost will come from the beneficiaries?
- Is this project the highest and best use of available funds given other needs in the community?

6. The Payback

- What will be the payback of solving this problem?

7. The Exit Strategy

- What is your exit strategy?

The **Seven Critical Questions** were created by Chris Jensen and Ted Boers in 2010 while attempting to increase crop productivity through irrigation techniques in Northwest Haiti.

68035343R00109

Made in the USA
Lexington, KY
29 September 2017